ALL ABOUT VARIABLE ANNUITIES

From the Inside Out

Bruce F. Wells

IRWIN
Professional Publishing®

Chicago ▪ Bogotá ▪ Boston ▪ Buenos Aires ▪ Caracas
London ▪ Madrid ▪ Mexico City ▪ Sydney ▪ Toronto

ISBN 1-55738-874-1

Printed in the United States of America

Q-K

1 2 3 4 5 6 7 8 9 0

Hendrickson Creative Communications

Once Again
To Suzanne

CONTENTS

PREFACE

All About Variable Annuities is a practical guide written for annuity investors, potential annuity investors, and investment professionals seeking a clear and concise understanding of one of the most dynamic investment opportunities of the 90s, the variable annuity.

Variable annuities offer investors the opportunity for wealth accumulation through the use of tax-deferral, professional asset management, asset allocation, diversification, and risk management. The book gives a straightforward and easily understood explanation of how variable (and fixed) annuities can be an integral part of a complete investment strategy to meet individual financial goals and objectives.

This book discusses the relationship between variable annuities and other types of investments including mutual funds, municipal bonds, equities, fixed income securities, and fixed annuities, and how they can be combined, through asset allocation, to produce consistent and competitive long-term investment returns while reducing risk.

The book is a complete guide to understanding variable annuities. It also presents information on retirement plans, retirement planning, three tier tax-advantaged investing, asset allocation, and the ten investment basics for gaining financial independence.

Whether a novice, experienced investor, or professional advisor, this book will give you the information, techniques, and investment strategies necessary for variable annuity investing and long-term tax-deferred wealth accumulation.

Bruce Franklin Wells

1

THE ANNUITY CONCEPT: AN OVERVIEW OF FIXED AND VARIABLE ANNUITIES

KEY CONCEPTS

▼ Long-Term Wealth Accumulation

▼ Tax-Deferred Compounding

▼ Professional Money Management

Present-day investors have a tremendous advantage over their predecessors. Advances in products, services, and investment strategies make it possible to design and implement financial plans for the most demanding customers and the most complex situations. Sophisticated computer programs, asset allocation models, and other leading-edge financial design technologies are now the tools of professional investment advisors. Furthermore, these advantages are available to individual investors for a relatively modest cost. Their systematic use can often double or triple an investor's long-term returns, compared to CDs and other guaranteed, fixed-income investments. This being the case, why aren't they more widely used by individuals? Why aren't we all rich instead of just beautiful?

Elementary, my dear Watson. Individual investors are exhausted from both the information overload and the tedious research required to implement a comprehensive, workable financial plan. Investors are also intimidated by computers, and even the most basic software can produce prodigious volumes of financial information. While education is power, especially when investing, this book offers an alternative to becoming an investment "techie" by presenting a commonsense approach to understanding variable annuities and to using that information to develop a total financial strategy that includes variable annuities.

This book is unabashedly written to encourage investors to consider the advantages of variable (and fixed) annuities for meeting long-term financial goals. However, before that decision can be made, an investor must understand that an annuity should be an important component of a total financial plan, not the entire financial plan.

Your first step in becoming investment planning and annuity "literate" is acquiring a general understanding of the history and the present, wonderful world of annuities.

Annuity Overview

Before Social Security and the widespread implementation of corporate and individual retirement plans, companies wishing to reward loyal employees would often "pension off" certain lucky individuals. Their lifetime retirement income was most often guaranteed by the purchase of an annuity. The annuity was also the investment of choice to provide for the "widows and orphans" of many dear departed breadwinners.

Everyone was happy. Employers were relieved of further financial responsibility, insurance companies provided lifetime incomes for a fee, and most recipients had the good manners to die reasonably quickly to avoid the problem of funding lengthy retirements. Widows and orphans survived on modest annuity incomes and the additional support of their families.

The system worked well until the country experienced some extraordinary social and economic changes. Our society moved from an agrarian to a manufacturing and service economy. Families provided less security. Employees looked to their employers for retirement income through "benefits packages." Average life expectancy grew dramatically, thus creating a greater need for retirement funding. Social Security was introduced to supplement retirement and family social needs.

The reengineered system worked well until recently when mergers, downsizing, and foreign and domestic competition eliminated many employment positions that provided job security and retirement benefits. This, in turn, caused mounting concern about funding individual retirements.

Fortunately, most retired or nearly retired individuals have various sources of funding their needs, including company pensions, Social Security benefits, savings, and various other investments.

Future generations may not be as fortunate. Out of necessity or opportunity many employers will reduce or eliminate retirement and medical benefits plans. Social Security will be reduced in real terms (buying power) despite the continued denials from Congress. The hard fact is that more individuals will be responsible for funding most of their own retirement.

Is purchasing a variable annuity the answer to funding one's retirement? If it is part of a wealth-accumulation strategy that includes qualified retirement plan contributions, short-term debt elimination, and other long-term investments the answer is, "Absolutely!"

If a person is retired and financially secure and wishes to defer taxes and build long-term wealth for whatever reasons, the answer is "Probably!" However, to make an informed decision requires knowledge and understanding about investments in general and variable annuities in particular. Let's start with the variable annuity. In its least descriptive form an annuity is a cash contract with an insurance company. Traditionally, it provides retirees a guaranteed, lifetime retirement income. The basic principle of an annuity is the systematic liquidation of its assets to provide that income.

There are two primary types of annuities: fixed and variable. A fixed annuity pays a guaranteed return (like a CD). A variable annuity's return is not guaranteed and depends on the performance of the underlying investments (like a mutual fund). The fixed annuity remains the annuity of choice for conservative investors, particularly retirees, when rates are competitive because of its predictability, stability, and guaranteed return.

To guarantee a fixed annuity return, the insurance company invests the fixed annuity premiums in conservative and stable securities. This strategy assures the investor that the insurance company will meet its contractual obligations. Thus, a fixed annuity's performance risk is assumed by the insurance company.

A variable annuity offers nonguaranteed investment choices, with an emphasis on equities (stocks). The variable accounts increase an investor's potential for higher returns while eliminating return guarantees and shifting the investment performance risk to the investor. Investing in fixed annuities increases during periods of high interest rates. Variable annuity purchases increase when fixed interest rates decline and/or investors are willing to assume risk in return for the opportunity of receiving a more competitive long-term return.

Two additional factors have contributed to the increased popularity of both fixed and variable annuities. First, investors are seeking relief from federal and state taxes that, combined, often exceed 50%. Second, annuity earnings grow tax-deferred.

In the classic sense, an annuity contract guarantees a fixed or variable rate for a specified time, usually for life. The contract owner makes lump-sum and/or periodic payments and receives a lump-sum or series of payments immediately or at a later date. In the modern sense, annuities are also investment vehicles incorporated into asset allocation and diversified portfolio strategies to meet retirement, wealth accumulation, and asset diversification requirements.

Fixed annuities are often compared to certificates of deposit (CDs). Each guarantees the return of principal and fixed interest rates for certain periods of time. CDs purchased from national and state banks are guaranteed by the FDIC. Annuities are guaranteed by the issuing insurance company's asset reserves. Annuities are not insured or guaranteed against loss by any federal or state agency.

Variable annuities are often called mutual funds with an insurance "wrapper." They offer investors numerous choices including a large selection of stock, bond, and money market sub-accounts (mutual funds).

Many otherwise well-informed and knowledgeable investors are unaware of fixed and variable annuity benefits. There are six critical points investors should know about annuities:

1. Tax-deferral and the "magic" of compounding are outstanding annuity benefits.
2. Consistent performance assures long-term wealth accumulation.
3. Annuity investors have access to world-class money managers.
4. Diversification through annuities reduces risk.
5. Annuities are long-term investments.
6. Owners control the tax and disbursement options of annuities.

Of all the annuity features, benefits, and options, the engine pulling the financial planning train is tax-deferred compounding. The Federal Tax Code allows tax deferral (inside buildup) on annuity earnings: that is, earnings are untaxed until disbursed. Disbursement may begin many years from the purchase date.

In emotional terms, tax deferral addresses an investor's abhorrence toward paying current income taxes. In absolute terms, it creates opportunities and investment alternatives for deferring taxes and meeting financial goals.

Sophisticated investors realize that wealth accumulation is the ultimate financial goal. They understand the necessity of providing for retirement and meeting long-term financial objectives. Consequently, those who take the long view are rewarded for their insight and sacrifice.

Access to professional money managers is another important benefit. Today's professional money managers have raised the investment decision-making process to a fine art. Their approach is comprehensive. Professional portfolio managers no longer simply select individual stocks and bonds. They now make short- and long-term economic predictions and strategic asset allocations based on current and projected interest rates, corporate earnings, macro- and micro-industry studies, general economic conditions, diversification, time horizon, risk tolerance, and expected investment returns.

Money managers then structure the portfolio to meet the sub-account's investment objective. Succinctly, professional money managers seek diversification, consistent performance, and competitive returns by maximizing a portfolio's return while assuming the minimum level of necessary risk.

Accountability is also essential to money management programs. Astute investors regularly review their portfolios to determine if their investment performance expectations are being met.

Thus, the major advantage of hiring professional money managers is apparent: Investors review and compare portfolio performance; they do not select individual securities, micromanage investments, or interpret the nuances of modern portfolio theory.

Most annuities are nonqualified investments. The Federal Tax Code sets no limits on annual nonsheltered annuity contributions. While nonqualified annuity contributions are not tax deductible and are made with after-tax dollars, earnings are untaxed until disbursed. This is particularly important to affluent investors paying current taxes on investments such as certificates of deposit and fixed-income mutual funds. They are using a short-term investment strategy to meet long-term wealth accumulation goals.

However, investors must also realize that annuities are long-term investments. Their money must be committed for an extended investment period, usually from 6 to 10 years, minimum. Otherwise, distributions can be subject to substantial early-withdrawal and, in certain situations, IRS penalties. Another annuity advantage, particularly for retirees, is that the tax liability on Social Security retirement benefits is eliminated during an annuity's deferral period. Unlike tax-free municipal bonds, annuity earnings are not included in the recipient's adjusted gross income (AGI) until the earnings are withdrawn. Concerns about liquidity—the ability to easily withdraw annuity assets—is another concern of investors. With some restrictions, most annuity contracts allow both systematic withdrawals and lump-sum distributions. Also, annuities pay the greater of the contract value or the principal value at the owner's death. Many contracts also reset the annuity's guaranteed value after a certain number of years.

Diversified investment programs that include annuities can be designed to meet most investment objectives. Combining retirement plans, variable annuities, fixed annuities, and municipal bonds can be particularly effective.

The Fixed Annuity

Fixed annuities have been one of the traditional insurance vehicles for funding retirement for millions of Americans. Their sales remain dominant over variable annuity sales although the gap is narrowing because conservative, long-term investors are now more willing to assume market risk. The major benefit of fixed annuities remains that, should an investor annuitize, the annuitant is assured a guaranteed lifetime income and cannot outlive the benefits. This, combined with a guaranteed interest rate, guaranteed return of principal, and tax-deferred wealth accumulation, has made fixed annuities attractive investments for many conservative and affluent investors.

Fixed annuities are the most like certificates of deposit and other types of bank savings programs. The principal is guaranteed and the interest rate is fixed for a specific period of time, usually one year or more. They are sold through most financial institutions, including insurance companies, banks, and brokerage firms. As with CDs, fixed annuity purchases are directly affected by the interest rate environment. They become less popular as interest rates fall (as in the early 1990s). Conversely, sales increase in direct proportion to rises in interest rates.

While purchases remain robust, particularly during times of competitive rates, three emerging factors have somewhat lessened investors' enthusiasm for fixed annuities: Because of inflation, their returns sometimes do not maintain purchasing power; over the long-term, equities outperform fixed-income portfolios; and many investors are now more willing to assume moderate risk as a conservative approach to long-term wealth accumulation.

The Variable Annuity

A variable annuity is a life insurance contract that is particularly well suited to assist investors in meeting long-term financial objectives. It combines the advantages of tax-deferred wealth accumulation with the flexibility and investment opportunities of mutual funds. All earnings and capital gains are tax-deferred; thus, the underlying investments grow more quickly than similar taxable investments. The corpus, consisting of the contributions, the accumulated interest and capital gains, and the money that would otherwise be paid in current taxes, continues to compound at an accelerating rate until either the money is either withdrawn or annuity payments begin.

Annuity owners control their contract options. They dictate the amount and regularity of their contributions, how their contributions are invested, and how and when the money is disbursed. The overriding benefit of both variable and fixed annuities is that they can guarantee a lifetime income.

Variable annuities are an integral part of many retirement investment strategies that combine employee-sponsored retirement savings programs and Social Security benefits. As with other long-term retirement programs, variable annuities have three phases: investment, accumulation, and disbursement.

In the investment phase, premiums are paid either lump-sum or periodically and are usually not subject to an initial sales charge. All proceeds are invested in sub-account portfolios of either stocks, bonds, or cash (money markets).

During the accumulation phase, earnings compound on a tax-deferred basis (inside buildup). They are not subject to taxation because of the reallocation of assets (switching).

The disbursement phase, as with all insurance contracts, offers the annuity owner numerous withdrawal options, including lifetime income, period and/or amount certain, and partial and full (lump-sum) disbursements.

The advantages of tax-deferred compounding cannot be overemphasized. Earnings not subject to current taxation can produce dramatic results. This, combined with the ability to reallocate assets without incurring a taxable event, makes variable annuities a highly competitive investment vehicle.

In addition to tax-deferred growth and owner control, other important benefits include professional money management, diversification, liquidity, and tax-liability selection alternatives.

The enormous growth of variable annuity purchases can be attributed to at least three major factors: investors seeking higher returns versus CDs, investors seeking relief from ever more burdensome federal and state taxes, and a growing recognition of the ability of professional money managers to deliver consistent and highly competitive returns to investors.

The explosive gains in variable annuity sales have been particularly beneficial to the average investor. The billions of dollars now being invested each year in variable annuities have convinced most major financial institutions that they want to participate in one of the fastest-growing segments of the investment market. With their involvement have come advantages traditionally available only to institutional investors—an enhanced level of investment service and state-of-the-art technologies that can custom-tailor portfolios to meet each investor's personal objectives.

Sub-accounts that cover all major asset classes are now available. Competition dictates that managers balance risk and return in their management styles and produce consistent, competitive returns. The abundance of sub-accounts offers the investor sufficient options to meet most investment needs. Asset allocation and diversification are available through the use of various sub-account investment options such as growth, international, fixed-income, high-yield, balanced, and equity income. Most variable annuities offer from 10 to 20 sub-account investment options. Sub-account exchanges do not create taxable events and have no sales and transfer charges, although some companies set limits on the number of annual exchanges before a transfer fee is charged.

Liquidity is another positive feature. Many annuities allow systematic withdrawals without penalty after the first year, subject to certain percentage restrictions. Unlike IRAs or other qualified retirement programs, there is no statutory age dictating the commencement of mandatory withdrawals. Both variable annuities and qualified retirement plans can be subject to early withdrawal and tax penalties.

The owner of an annuity selects the beneficiary, annuitant, and/or contingent owner and may change either or all during the accumulation phase. The owner also determines when distributions commence and in what combination(s). This allows the owner to determine his or her own tax consequences. Finally, when the owner dies, the corpus of the annuity passes directly to the designated beneficiary without passing through probate.

Summary

- There are two types of annuities, fixed and variable. The insurance company assumes the risk for a fixed annuity by guaranteeing both the interest rate and the return of principal. The variable annuity risk is assumed by the investor in return for the opportunity to receive a higher return from nonguaranteed investments, primarily equities.
- Both variable and fixed annuities offer tax-deferred wealth accumulation, professional money management, owner control, liquidity, lifetime income options, safety, avoidance of probate, and guaranteed death benefits.
- Combined taxation by federal and state governments has made annuities more attractive than ever because of their tax-advantaged features and benefits. Contributions to purchase nonqualified annuities are not tax-deductible, there is no contribution limitation, and assets grow tax-deferred until withdrawn. Finally, there is no age requirement at which distributions must begin.
- As more and more American workers realize that they are responsible for funding their own retirement, they find that annuities, combined with corporate retirement plans, Social Security benefits, and savings, make an excellent combination for meeting those retirement needs.

- Certificates of deposit remain the investment of choice for many savers and investors. While guaranteeing return of principal and the interest rate, CDs often do not address the biggest long-term investor risk: loss of purchasing power through inflation.
- Fixed annuities remain the choice for the majority of annuity buyers. Like CDs, they guarantee the return of principal and interest rate. Their downside is that fixed annuities do not always yield highly competitive "net" real returns. Variable annuity returns are not guaranteed, but address the issue of inflation.

2

THE MAJOR FEATURES AND BENEFITS OF THE VARIABLE ANNUITY

KEY CONCEPTS

▼ Tax-Deferred Wealth Accumulation

▼ Investment Flexibility

▼ Investor Control

▼ Annuity Guarantees

Annuities are leading-edge investments. Their suitability for meeting long-term financial goals is best determined by well-informed investors possessing the knowledge necessary to make logical, unemotional decisions. The decision to invest in an annuity should be calculated and straightforward. Comparing different variable annuities is appropriate. Consider their individual features and benefits. Finally, a variable annuity should be a component of a diversified investment strategy, not the total plan.

Our emphasis remains variable annuities, but fixed annuities also offer benefits. Remember, the major difference between fixed and variable annuities is that a fixed annuity offers a guaranteed return, while a variable annuity's return depends on the nonguaranteed performance of the underlying securities.

Major Benefits

Tax-Deferred Wealth Accumulation

An annuity's earnings accumulate tax-deferred; thus, contributions, earnings, and money ordinarily taken by taxes remain in the account and continue to grow. Capital gains and dividends are automatically reinvested without current federal, state, or local taxation.

This triple compounding through tax deferral produces a return on all invested money. Triple compounding means you earn:

1. Capital gains and interest on the principal;
2. Capital gains and interest on the earnings;
3. Capital gains and interest on the money you normally lose to taxes.

Does tax-deferred wealth accumulation make a difference? Table 2–1 demonstrates the results.

Flexibility

Fixed annuity investment options are straightforward and limited. The two primary decisions are selecting a maturity date and accepting the interest rate. As with CDs, the fixed annuity interest rates are a function of the fixed-income markets. Fixed annuities offer either 1-year guaranteed rates with annual renewals or interest rate guarantee periods ranging from 1 to 10 years, depending on the issuer. Guarantees of 1, 2, 3, 5, 7, and 10 years are common. One-year rates are the industry standard.

Table 2–1. $100,000 Investment Compounded Over Ten Years

End of Year	10% Tax Deferred	5% Net Taxable
1	$110,000	$105,000
2	121,000	110,250
3	133,100	115,763
4	146,410	121,551
5	161,051	127,628
6	177,156	134,010
7	194,872	140,710
8	214,359	147,746
9	235,795	155,133
10	259,374	162,889
$100,000 compounded at 10% for ten years		$259,374
$100,000 compounded at 5% for ten years		162,889
Difference		96,485

Variable annuity options are more diverse. Contracts offering 10 to 20 sub-accounts, from aggressive growth to money markets, are common. Some variable annuities even offer fixed sub-accounts similar to fixed annuities.

Reallocation of Assets

An annuity owner has the ability to reallocate (switch) assets between sub-accounts to change an asset allocation mix without creating a taxable event or being subject to commission charges. This is a definite advantage when compared to other investment events, as shown in Table 2–2.

Table 2–2. Taxable Events for Various Financial Transactions

Event	Gain/Loss/Income Recognized
Sale of Stock	Time of Sale
Dividend/Interest Paid	Time of Payment
Sale of Mutual Fund	Time of Sale
Sale of Security in IRA	When Withdrawn from Account*
Annuity Sub-Account Switch	When Withdrawn from Account*
Fixed Annuity Interest Paid	When Withdrawn from Account*

*No taxable event occurs until withdrawn from the account

*Transfers and switches are not taxable events

No Sales Charges (No Front-End Load)

You will incur no front-load sales charges (commissions) on most variable annuity purchases—100% of the money invested earns an immediate return. However, a contingent deferred sales charge (CDSC) may be assessed for early surrender.

Investment Note: Withdrawal penalties are usually based on the purchase payments only, from time of purchase.

A typical surrender charge schedule is shown in Table 2–3.

Surrender Penalties Versus Free Withdrawals

Most annuities provide systematic and periodic withdrawal options to annuity investors. These withdrawals are not subject to surrender penalties unless they exceed certain withdrawal limitations or restrictions.

Variable annuity distribution options vary widely, but many have common features including:

1. Minimum account value to qualify for a withdrawal option.
2. Minimum withdrawal amount for each distribution.

Table 2–3. Typical Surrender Charge Schedule

Years Since Deposit	1	2	3	4	5	6	7	7+
Charge	7%	6%	5%	4%	3%	2%	1%	0%

Example: An investor purchases a $100,000 annuity and surrenders it for redemption after three years, assuming a 10% compounded return.

Purchase Price	$100,000
1st year net earnings	10,000
2nd year net earnings	11,000
3rd year net earnings	12,100
Three-Year Account Value	$133,100
Less 4% withdrawal penalty*	($4,000)
Net Redemption Value	$129,100

*Based on contributions only

3. Maximum number of withdrawals per contract year.
4. Withdrawal will be deducted proportionally from each subaccount unless otherwise directed.
5. Each withdrawal is subject to federal income taxes on the taxable portion.
6. A 10% penalty may be assessed on withdrawals if you are under age 59 1/2 (IRS penalty).
7. Withdrawals may be modified or discontinued at any time prior to annuitization.

Guaranteed Death Benefit

An annuity is an insurance policy. Proceeds are paid to a beneficiary in the event of the annuity owner's death prior to the annuitization date. The amount paid to the beneficiary is always at least 100% of the investor's purchase payments (total of funds invested) less prior withdrawals and prior applicable surrender charges. At the death of the annuity owner, all future surrender penalties are waived, regardless of the time of ownership. Consider the following examples.

Example 1: An investor purchases a $100,000 variable annuity and selects an aggressive, sub-account portfolio. Six months after the purchase the annuity owner dies. Because of a market decline, the accumulation account's value at the time of his death is $90,000. The beneficiary receives $100,000, which is 100% of the invested funds. Should the value of the accumulation account exceed the value of the purchase payments, the greater amount will be received by the beneficiary.

Example 2: An investor purchases a $100,000 variable annuity. Three years later the annuity owner dies. The beneficiary receives $135,000, the account's value at the time of death.

Many variable annuities offer an adjusted guaranteed minimum death benefit. It guarantees the beneficiary will receive an adjusted amount (step-up) that reflects the value of the accumulation account after a certain period of time, usually five or more years.

Example 3: An investor purchases a $100,000 variable annuity. After five years the portfolio value is $150,000 and the guaranteed benefit is adjusted to a $150,000 minimum. Six months later the annuity owner dies. The annuity value at time of his death is $140,000. The beneficiary receives $150,000, despite total contributions being $100,000 and the account value being $140,000 at the time of the owner's death.

Avoids Probate

At the death of the owner, the annuity contract value will transfer to the designated beneficiary or the joint owner without probate. There are no delays and the beneficiary receives immediate access to the proceeds. If the beneficiary is the surviving spouse of the owner, the spouse may assume contract ownership and continue the contract as if the owner had not died.

The Federal Tax Code sets certain distribution requirements for beneficiaries other than spouses:

1. If the annuity owner dies prior to the annuity date, the proceeds must be distributed within five years following the owner's death.
2. If the annuity owner dies on or after the annuity date, but before the entire interest in the contract has been distributed, the remaining interest must be distributed at least as rapidly as under the method of distribution being used at the time of the death of the owner.

Both these requirements are considered met if:

1. The portion of the proceeds is payable to the beneficiary over a period not exceeding his or her life expectancy.
2. Distributions begin within one year after the death of the previous owner.

Investment Note: While the beneficiary inherits the annuity proceeds tax-free, the value of the annuity is still included in the estate of the deceased for federal estate tax purposes. All states allow the direct transfer of annuity assets to the beneficiary.

Distribution Options

There are a number of distribution-at-death options available to owners of nonqualified annuity contracts. They require ownership, annuitant, and beneficiary designations by the annuity owner.

The most prominent distribution options are as follows:

1. Lump-Sum Distribution: The contract owner withdraws the entire annuity value in one payment.
2. Lifetime Income: The contract owner "annuitizes" the contract and receives an income for life.
3. Lifetime Income With Period Certain: The owner "annuitizes" the contract and receives an income for life and a guarantee that a certain number of payments will be made even if he/she dies prematurely.
4. Systematic Withdrawals: The owner determines his/her distribution needs and systematically withdraws that amount without annuitizing the contract.
5. No Withdrawals: The contract owner makes no withdrawals, lets the assets grow tax-deferred until his/her death, and passes the money directly to the beneficiary.

Safety

The preservation of capital and the return of capital are major concerns of investors. Annuities guarantee that the beneficiary will receive either the original principal amount invested (less withdrawals), the current market value of the account, or the guaranteed "stepped-up" value, whichever is greater, at the contract owner's death.

Fixed annuities are backed by the full faith and credit of the issuing insurance company. The insurance company must meet certain reserve requirements established by the various state insurance commissions. The insurance company may invest only in certain types of investments in order to preserve the integrity for the reserve accounts. In addition, the annuity portfolios are monitored by the various state insurance commissions.

Variable annuities are backed by the full faith and credit of the issuing company, but have an additional safety feature: the securities for the underlying portfolios (sub-accounts) in which the annuitant invests are held by a trustee.

The strict regulations required by the various state insurance commissions assure annuity owners that their principal and earnings are protected and that their annuity contractual obligations will be met. (See Table 2–4.)

Liquidity

Since an annuity is subject to certain distribution restrictions and penalties for early redemption, the availability of assets to meet emergency needs is often the dominant concern of annuity investors. To address these concerns, annuities offer a wide range of penalty-free distribution options to meet any financial crisis:

1. After one year, cumulative earnings can be withdrawn without penalty.
2. After one year, all or part of the accumulated earnings or up to 10% of the total account value, whichever is greater, may be withdrawn.
3. A systematic withdrawal plan to meet monthly financial needs. (Usually subject to minimum payment amounts and a minimum duration of 12 months.)

It is important to again emphasize that withdrawals of gains are taxed at ordinary income rates and can also be subject to a 10% federal penalty tax if made prior to the contract owner reaching age 59 1/2.

Table 2–4. Comparable Insurance Company Ratings

Standard & Poor's	A. M. Best	Moody's Investor
AAA	A+	Aaa
AA+	Contingent A+	Aa1
AA	A & Contingent A	Aa2
AA–	A–	Aa3
A+	Contingent A–	AA1
A	B+	A2
A–	Contingent B+	A2
BBB+	B	Baa1
BBB	Contingent B	Baa2
BBB–	B–	Baa3

Major Features

Section 1035 Tax-Free Exchanges

Code Section 1035 generally provides that no gain or loss shall be recognized on the exchange of one annuity contract for another. Therefore an owner may exchange one contract for another without creating a taxable event.

Some considerations for annuity exchange are:

1. Invest in an annuity that offers a more competitive and/or diversified program.
2. Increase the guaranteed death benefit of the annuity.
3. Transfer to an insurance company with more stability and creditworthiness.

Some disadvantages of switching are (could be):

1. The transfer being subject to early withdrawal penalties.
2. Again making the transferred assets subject to surrender charges.

Investment Note: To discourage transfers of annuities no longer subject to surrender penalties, many insurance companies now include a "step-up" guaranteed-death-benefit provision in their annuity policies.

Free-Look Period

Annuity contracts include a "right to examine" provision that allows the contract owner a certain period of time to cancel the contract, usually 10 days or longer, depending on the individual state's legal requirements and regulations. Should the purchaser decide to cancel, in most states he or she will receive the greater of the purchase price or the value of the accumulation account, less certain charges for mortality and expense risk charges, administration fees, and state taxes.

Social Security Income Exclusion

Social Security retirement income may be subject to federal income tax when Social Security benefits are added to other income and the amount exceeds certain limits. Among revenue sources included in other income are earned income, dividends, capital gains, interest, and tax-free interest. The limits are:

1. Single $25,000
2. Married filing joint $32,000
3. Head of household $25,000
4. Qualifying widow(er) $25,000

Nondistributed annuity earnings are not included in any Social Security taxation calculations. This allows Social Security recipients to continue accumulating tax-deferred wealth in their annuities without creating a taxable event.

Investor Control

Investors are most concerned with having sufficient assets to maintain a reasonable lifestyle after retirement. Annuities offer investors the opportunity to accumulate wealth, the ability to maintain control over those assets, and the final decision on the distribution of those assets. The owner (annuitant) of the contract determines the amount of the contribution, the investment vehicle(s), the asset allocation model, the investment time period, when and how the assets are disbursed, and who receives the assets at the annuitant's death (beneficiary).

This is an important feature, as most investors insist upon control of their assets.

Professional Money Management

The assets of the variable annuity sub-accounts are managed by some of the most qualified and successful professional money managers available. They offer investors access to institutional management, competitive and consistent returns over the long term, and the assurance of expert oversight. Each sub-account is managed to meet a specific investment objective. An investor can choose between aggressive growth, growth, balanced, fixed-income, and money market sub-accounts to develop as diversified a portfolio as required. The investor can also be assured that the manager of each sub-account seeks to maximize the investment for the least amount of risk possible to meet the objective.

Unlimited Contributions

Unlike retirement plans, contributions for the purchase of an annuity are not limited by federal statute. Conversely, no portion of the annuity contribution is tax deductible. This is an attractive feature for affluent investors seeking to defer income until either their income has declined or they wish to pass the proceeds to a beneficiary while avoiding probate.

Summary

- Variable annuities are leading-edge investments offering investors an outstanding opportunity for tax-deferred wealth accumulation with triple compounding.
- Variable annuities offer investors many additional benefits, including no sales charges, probate avoidance, guaranteed death benefits, and numerous distribution options.
- Variable annuities offer double safety through the full faith and credit of the issuing insurance company and the trustee-ship of all sub-account assets.
- Numerous liquidity options are available. This can be very important to retirees seeking a systematic withdrawal of their assets.
- Investors may switch from one annuity contract to another with a Section 1035 exchange without incurring a taxable event.
- Annuity contracts include the right to a free-look period of at least 10 days.
- Deferred earnings from annuities are not included in Social Security benefit calculations unless received.
- Annuity investors have access to the world's greatest money managers.
- There are no contribution limits on annuities, nor is any portion of the contribution tax-deductible.

3

THE TEN INVESTMENT BASICS FOR GAINING FINANCIAL INDEPENDENCE

KEY CONCEPTS

▼ Inflation and the Consumer Price Index (CPI)

▼ Acceptable Risk and Investing

▼ The Importance of Time in Investing

▼ The "Magic" of Compounding

▼ Consistent Investment Performance

Realistic Expectations

There are three financial truths: The overriding goal of most investors is financial independence; each investor has the opportunity to make his or her money grow at competitive rates; and most people have very little idea how to manage their assets effectively.

Achieving a comfortable, secure financial status is not necessarily easy unless one has the good fortune to be born to the manor, win the lottery, marry an affluent and generous mate, or is just plain lucky. Otherwise, one's choices are those of most other bright but initially broke individuals: work, sacrifice, save, and invest. They're tedious, but they're the only choices until something better comes along.

How does one become financially independent? As in achieving any goal, an investor must understand the rules, participate, and make the commitment necessary to win the game. An important step is to become investment "literate." An uninformed investor is most often doomed to either mediocrity or failure. Understanding investment techniques and strategies need not be complicated, convoluted,or difficult. If it were, many highly successful investment advisory industry employees would be otherwise engaged. My experience has been that the most successful money mangers employ conservative, proven, basic investment strategies blended with good old-fashioned common sense.

What has being investment "literate" to do with purchasing an annuity? Everything.

Let's immediately understand the role of an annuity for investors. As previously stated, an annuity should be part of a total investment strategy, not *the* investment strategy. So let's review some of the basic knowledge necessary to become an educated, confident investor. This, in turn, will assist an investor in making an informed decision when purchasing an annuity.

The initial step in developing a long-term investment strategy is to determine an investor's net worth by completing a personal "balance sheet."

Equally important is interpreting the subjective information that relates to an investor's attitude toward risk, expected return, and specific types of investments. Having an "attitude" is not always bad.

Evaluating qualitative (subjective) information begins with understanding one's own demographics. The stereotypical investor is really not an investor, but a saver. By definition, investors willingly assume risk. Savers seldom willingly accept risk or understand that investing requires persistence, planning, and professional guidance. From an emotional perspective, savers are comfortable with guaranteed interest rates and guaranteed return of principal. Few envision purchasing-power loss caused by inflation as a major risk or realize that the benefits of tax-advantaged wealth accumulation strategies are important.

Placing a disproportionate importance on the preservation of capital and guaranteed returns satisfies a saver's emotional goal of risk avoidance. However, it eliminates the opportunity of receiving competitive, consistent returns. Including risk within acceptable constraints to capture a competitive total return is an appropriate balance.

So, investor, study the following investment basics.

First Basic:
Inflation and Real Rates of Return

An investor's real return is the total return adjusted for inflation, as measured by the Consumer Price Index (CPI). After-tax and after-inflation returns on risk-free investments often give savers net negative returns. This has created a growing demand for more competitive and creative investments for sophisticated investors willing to accept equity and fixed-income market risk to meet their financial objectives.

Understanding the different types of returns is also important:

Total Return: Annual return on an investment including gains (losses) and dividends and interest.

Negative Net Return: If the net return on an investment is less than the inflation rate, the saver or investor has lost purchasing power.

Positive Net Return: If the net return on an investment is more than the inflation rate, the saver or investor has gained purchasing power.

The importance of receiving a net positive return cannot be overemphasized. The biggest risk a long-term investor faces is loss of purchasing power, not market risk, as illustrated in Table 3–1.

Now that you are becoming a financial genius, you have more basics to cover before we end this chapter and you graduate with honors. Let's discuss some subjective investor concerns. While investors view their financial circumstances as unique, most share common goals. Their overriding concerns include:

1. Having an adequate monthly retirement income;
2. Market risk involving their investments;
3. Depletion of assets for retirement living expenses;
4. Liquidity for major emergencies.

We already know these concerns are legitimate because we understand inflation. However, since these concerns are based on emotion not quantitative (measurable) standards, how can they be addressed? Again, knowledge, stability, and common sense are the necessary tools.

Second Basic: Understanding and Accepting Risk to Meet Financial Goals

The issue of investment risk and reward is more fully discussed in the money management portion of this book. For our immediate purposes, the following investment knowledge regarding risk is important:

1. An investor must accept a degree of risk in order to receive a more competitive return.
2. As an investment time period expands, the adverse effects of a negative event dissipate.
3. Risk is reduced through diversification, asset allocation, and time.

Table 3–1. What Is an Investor's Real Return on a $10,000 CD Yielding 5%?

Total Annual Interest Received	$500
Less 28% taxes paid (assumption)	(140)
Net Cash Received	$360
4% inflation rate (assumption)	(400)
Loss of Purchasing Power	($40)

Note:	The investor has lost purchasing power, not actual cash.
Example of inflation:	A new luxury car cost $4,000 in 1960. How much will you pay for one today?

The bottom line for investors? By accepting a degree of risk over a long-term period, they receive a more competitive return. In essence, by assuming risk, savers modify their strategy and become investors. This is not for the faint of heart or those set in their ways, but it is an essential ingredient to becoming financially independent.

Third Basic:
The Importance of Time in Investing

Becoming an investor and funding investment programs to meet retirement, education, and other goals need not be difficult, and the reward of financial independence is obvious. There are two investment absolutes regarding time that make funding less complicated and dramatically increase the opportunity for success.

First, the earlier a person starts investing, the earlier he or she will gain financial independence. Second, combining systematic investing with a long-term horizon will meet most investment goals through compounding. There is a clear distinction between short-term and long-term investing. All investments contain a degree of risk if the return is subject to variation. Hence, time horizons are especially important to an understanding of market risk factors.

Market fluctuations have a more dramatic effect on security prices over a short-term period, and their values may vary substantially. Over longer time periods the effect of specific events and general market conditions on security prices dissipates.

Variable and fixed annuities are long-term investments. Many traditional investors continue to use short-term investment vehicles to meet long-term investment objectives. The key to success is to identify long-term goals and select investment vehicles that meet them. Variable annuity investors select from three asset classes: fixed-income, equities, and cash. Over the longer term, equities have produced superior investment results. Over the shorter term, equities have consistently demonstrated a higher risk exposure than short-term fixed-income returns.

While volatility is important to investors, inflation is equally important. The main objective of any investor is to maintain purchasing power by receiving net investment returns that exceed the inflation rate (CPI).

Fourth Basic:
The Magic of Compounding

Substantial wealth accumulation requires longer time periods. The "magic of compounding" and small, annual, positive differences in investment returns become extremely important in wealth accumulation over longer time periods. Annuities offer the opportunity for tax-deferred wealth accumulation through long-term compounding as shown in Table 3–2.

Fifth Basic:
Consistent Investment Performance

Reasonably consistent investment performance is essential for both wealth accumulation and strategic financial planning. Various investments, including variable annuity portfolios (sub-accounts), experience differing performance returns and degrees of volatility, depending on the allocation of assets within the portfolio.

Investors generally are most comfortable with a conservative approach to wealth accumulation and include the preservation of capital as an equally important consideration. Therefore, when designing a portfolio that includes annuities and other investments, a conservative approach is always recommended.

As demonstrated by Tables 3–3, 3–4, and 3–5, consistent performance is a major ingredient in investment success. Equally important, it also provides preservation of capital.

Sixth Basic: Realistic
Expectations and Accountability

There is no free lunch for investors. The certificate of deposit buyer's interest rate and return of principal are guaranteed. The counterbalance is the possible erosion of purchasing power and the lost opportunity for capital appreciation.

The saver's antithesis, the speculator, accepts a high degree of risk in anticipation of a high return. If successful, double-digit investment returns are common. If unsuccessful, the loss of investment capital can be significant.

The most successful investors balance an anticipated return with an acceptable level of risk, seek competitive and consistent performance, reduce risk through diversification, and maintain a portfolio that addresses the appropriate time horizon.

Table 3–2

| Example | $100,000 compounded at 8% and 10% for 10 years |
| | $100,000 distributing all earnings for 10 years |

Year End	Total Amount 8% Compounding	Total Amount 10% Compounding	Total Amount 10% Simple Interest*
1	$108,000	$110,000	$110,000
2	116,640	121,000	120,000
3	125,971	133,100	130,000
4	136,049	146,410	140,000
5	146,933	161,051	150,000
6	158,687	177,156	160,000
7	171,382	194,872	170,000
8	185,093	214,359	180,000
9	199,900	235,795	190,000
10	215,892	259,374	200,000

* Distribute interest each year.

Unsophisticated investors often have unrealistic investment return expectations. They seek high fixed rates and anticipate substantial capital appreciation, but are unwilling to accept market risk to achieve those potential gains. Again, a reality check is in order. Seeking additional returns will always require increasing risk (additional market exposure) in an efficient portfolio. You can take that to the bank.

How can you tell if you are doing well? Sophisticated investors measure performance over specific time horizons. The results are compared to indices, peer performance, and other asset classes. The comparison will indicate if the portfolio is producing the anticipated results for the level of risk inherent to the portfolio and if the returns are competitive.

Table 3–3. Consistent versus Volatile Portfolio Comparison

Assumption: $1,000,000 portfolio compounding for five years with an average return of 10% for each portfolio.

	Year 1	Year 2	Year 3	Year 4	Year 5	Total Return
Consistent	10%	10%	10%	10%	10%	$1,610,510
Volatile	20%	(40%)	50%	(30%)	50%	1,134,000

Table 3–4. Calculations: Consistent Portfolio

Year	Initial Investment	Annual Percent	Annual Return	Principal + Earned Interest
1	$1,000,000	10%	$100,000	$1,100,000
2		10%	110,000	1,210,000
3		10%	121,000	1,331,000
4		10%	133,110	1,464,100
5		10%	146,410	1,610,510
Average Compounded Rate		10%		

Seventh Basic:
Investment Building Blocks

Most investors lack the expertise to manage their personal assets in a manner that maximizes their return for the level of risk taken. This lack of knowledge, combined with another hindrance, procrastination, creates an atmosphere in which investors are often doomed to either mediocrity or failure.

The approach to successful investing is straightforward. The building blocks are knowledge, discipline, consistency, and time horizon. The capstone is realistic expectations. Knowledge gives an investor the ability to clearly define specific financial goals and objec-

Table 3–5. Calculations: Volatile Portfolio

Year	Initial Investment	Annual Percent	Annual Return	Principal + Earned Interest
1	$1,000,000	20%	$200,000	$1,200,000
2		(40%)	(480,000)	720,000
3		50%	360,000	1,080,000
4		(30%)	(324,000)	756,000
5		50%	378,000	1,134,000
Average Compounded Rate		10%		

tives. Discipline demands that the investor continue "full steam ahead" in both prosperous and difficult environments. Consistency requires regular contributions, diversification of assets, and monitoring investment results. Time is the most significant ingredient in successful financial planning. First, as the time horizon expands, the total dollar contribution demands decrease. Second, the "magic of compounding" benefits exponentially from expanding time horizons.

Eighth Basic: The Cornerstone of Investing—Dollar-Cost Averaging

Dollar-cost-averaging is the technique of investing a fixed sum at regular intervals regardless of stock or bond market movements.* This reduces average share costs to the investor, who acquires more shares in periods of lower prices and fewer shares in periods of higher prices. This spreads investment risk over time.

Many investors build their portfolios through the systematic purchase of securities called dollar-cost averaging. It is the cornerstone of many investment programs. The method dictates that the investor

---

* Source: *Barron's Dictionary of Finance and Investment Terms.*

purchase fixed dollar amounts of sub-accounts (or mutual funds) at regular intervals, without regard to price. When prices are high, fewer shares are purchased. Conversely, when prices are low, more shares are purchased. The net result is that the average cost of all sub-account units (shares) bought is lower than the average of all the prices at which the purchases were made.

A program stressing this approach is a good long-term investment strategy. It does not guarantee that the investor will always have profits; it does, however, reduce risk.

Average Price Versus Average Cost

By investing equal amounts over a period of time, the average cost paid for sub-account units (shares) is lower than the average paid (see Table 3–6).

Ninth Basic: Time Value of Money

Understanding the time value of money, the future value of a present sum (compounding), and the present value of a future sum (discounting) is beneficial for any investor.

The principal behind the time value of money is that a dollar received today and has more value than a dollar received in the future; conversely, a dollar received in the future is worth less than a dollar received today. The principal is straightforward. The recipient may invest a dollar received today start earning immediately. Investing a future dollar is delayed until it is received; therefore, it has less value than one received today.

Calculating the time value of money has some very practical applications. You can figure how much money must be invested today (lump sum) or monthly (periodic payments) to fund a college education in 10 years or calculate how inflation will affect the dollar (purchasing power) during the next 10 years if the annual inflation rate (CPI) is 6%.

Table 3–6. Average Price vs. Average Cost

Assume $2,000 a month invested for six months. The total investment is $12,000.

Price	Units Purchased
$20	100
18	111
16	125
14	143
16	125
18	111
102	715

Total cost of $12,000/715 = $16.78 per Unit average cost.
Average purchase price $102/6 = $17.00 per Unit price.
(Total Prices/Total Purchases)

Present Value Illustration

The practical application for fixed and variable annuity investors is that, with reasonable assurance, the future value of an annuity can be calculated. For example, how much money must you invest today to have $100,000 in 10 years if your money compounds at 10%?

Refer to Table 3–7. The applicable years and percent intersect at 0.38554. In other words, to receive $1.00 in 10 years, invest $0.38554. To receive $100,000 in 10 years, invest $38,554.

Another example is calculating. How much equivalent buying power will $10,000 have if inflation averages 6% for the next 10 years? Refer again to Table 3–7. The applicable years and percent intersect at 0.55839. The present-day purchasing power of $1.00 in ten years will be $0.55839. The present day purchasing power of $10,000 in ten years will be $5,583.90. This demonstrates the biggest risk for all investors: inflation.

Table 3–7. Present Value of $1.00

Years	6%	7%	8%	9%	10%
5	0.74726	0.71299	0.68058	0.64993	0.62092
6	0.70496	0.66634	0.63017	0.59627	0.56447
7	0.66506	0.62275	0.58349	0.54703	0.51316
8	0.62741	0.58201	0.54027	0.50187	0.46651
9	0.59190	0.54393	0.50025	0.46043	0.42410
10	0.55839	0.50835	0.46319	0.42241	0.38554

Future Value Illustration

Systematic (periodic) investing is a widely used variable annuity funding method. Rather than a lump-sum payment, we assume an annual contribution of $1,000 for 10 years. How much is the value of the annuity if it compounds at 10%? See Table 3–8.

Investment Note: Complete present value, future value, and future value of an annuity tables are available in any basic financial management college text or financial management computer software.

Table 3–8. Future Value of an Annuity

Years	8%	9%	10%
8	10.637	11.028	11.436
9	12.488	13.021	13.579
10	14.487	15.193	15.937

Illustration: The future value of a $1,000 payment per year for 10 years, compounded at 10%, is $15,937. Go to applicable years/percent intersect, in this case 15.937. Total contributions: $10,000; total earnings: $5,937.

Tenth Basic: Measuring Investment Returns (Benchmarks)

A friend states, "I'm really doing well. Last year my equity mutual fund earned 12%." How well is your friend really doing? It depends on the fund's performance versus similar funds and versus an index selected for comparison.

Mutual funds and sub-accounts are compared to other similar funds and ranked according to performance by various rating services. For example: say there are 60 similar mutual funds. The fund's performance rank is 10 among 60. The average return for the 60 funds was 11.02%; our fund earned 12%. We now have the answer—the fund is doing well.

Funds and sub-accounts are also compared to indices to judge performance. Say our fund invests primarily in blue-chip stocks. The index chosen for performance comparison is the Dow Jones Industrial Average (DJIA). The DJIA appreciated in value by 9.7% for our time period. Our 12.0% return for the same period compares favorably to the DJIA's increase of 9.7%. Again, it confirms that our fund is doing well.

There are different benchmarks for different types of subaccounts and mutual funds. A broader range of stocks might be compared to the Standard & Poor's 500 Stock Average (S&P 500). Fixed-income securities are compared to fixed-income indices. The purpose is to judge performance relative to a peer group and/or an index that measures a specific "market," such as growth stocks or government bond funds.

This is important to investors. Only by comparison can we judge how we are doing.

Summary

- Before an investor purchases an annuity or any other type of investment, he or she should understand the basics of investing. This includes risk, return, consistent performance, compounding, and realistic investment return expectations.
- Time is the single most important ingredient for successful investing. It dissipates short-term risk, allows compounding to work, and reasonably assures that long-term financial goals will be reached.
- The biggest risk every investor faces is inflation and loss of purchasing power, not market risk.
- The cornerstone of many mutual fund and sub-account investing programs is dollar-cost averaging. This long-term strategy does not guarantee profits, but it does build wealth while reducing risks with a systematic approach to investing.
- The time value of money is another critical ingredient in successful investing.
- Compounding and discounting are bedrock principals of financial planning strategies. Their use greatly enhances the opportunity for wealth accumulation.
- You can't really tell how much financial progress you are making unless you have a method for measuring progress. By comparing a sub-account or mutual fund's performance to a peer group or applicable indices, an evaluation is possible.

4

VARIABLE ANNUITY SUB-ACCOUNTS

To Purchase an Annuity or Not?

The colorful brochures of the insurance companies depict mature couples sailing yachts or playing golf and tennis at major resorts. It's a great image and absolutely true for the fortunate few. However, the reality is that most investors purchase annuities and accumulate tax-deferred capital to meet the daily living expenses of retirement, not to buy yachts and sail to Bora Bora.

Making an informed decision to purchase an annuity is not complicated, but it does require knowledge. Ideally, the decision is made by an investor who understands investment objectives, time horizons, risk tolerances, the basics of asset allocation and the investment objectives of the annuity's sub-accounts.

The commitment to purchase a variable annuity is the easiest component of the investment decision-making process. The initial investment commitment requires two straightforward decisions: how much money will be invested and how will the purchase be made, as a lump sum or as a series of payments?

Once the purchase decision is made, an investor must make a subsequent determination on where to invest annuity contributions. There are no absolute rules, but the variables remain investment objective, time horizon, and risk tolerance when selecting appropriate sub-accounts.

For those unduly concerned about selecting the appropriate sub-accounts there is solace in the pioneering and Nobel Prize–winning economic efforts of Dr. Harry M. Markowitz. His 1959 work, *Portfolio Selection and Efficient Diversification of Investments*, stresses that individual securities transactions are important only to the extent that they affect the risk-return relationship of the total portfolio. That is, investors should select good money managers, not individual securities.

Thanks to the pioneering work of Dr. Markowitz and the subsequent work of Dr. William F. Sharpe, the sub-account selection process is relatively simple. Sub-account managers select individual securities for the sub-accounts; the investor then selects the most appropriate sub-accounts for his or her portfolio.

Sound exactly like your mutual fund investments? That's because it *is* exactly like your mutual fund investments. Investors choose mutual funds primarily because of their professional money management, convenience, and economies of scale. Succinctly, sub-accounts are mutual funds within an insurance contract and are chosen as investment vehicles for the same reasons mutual funds are chosen, with the added benefit of tax-deferred wealth accumulation. Mutual fund features and benefits remain the same, even when they are called sub-accounts.

What's in a name? Mutual funds are usually identified by their investment company (mutual fund company) and their primary investment objective and/or primary group of securities, such as Spectacular U. S. Government Bond Fund or Spectacular Aggressive Growth Fund.

Sub-accounts include the name of their primary investment objective and/or their primary group of securities, but also include the name of the issuing insurance company, the mutual fund company and/or the investment advisor managing the assets, and the fund's investment objective. Examples include, Wild Life of Arkansas Insurance Company/Benton Asset Management/U. S. Government Bond Fund.

A more descriptive name for a variable annuity sub-account is necessary to understand its structure. Most investment companies (mutual fund companies) employ in-house money managers to manage their family of mutual funds.

Managing the assets of an insurance company's variable annuity sub-accounts can be more complex. Insurance companies employ one or more of four distinct strategies when managing sub-account assets:

1. Manage all sub-accounts internally.

Example: Assets are managed by money managers employed by the insurance company.

2. Engage an independent investment advisor group as money manager for all sub-accounts.

Example: Arkansas Life employs Southeast Capital Management as money manager for all sub-accounts.

    3. Employ multiple independent advisors who specialize in a specific investment area to manage a specific sub-account(s).

Example: Arkansas Life employs Southeast Capital Management to manage all equity sub-accounts and Pensacola Asset Management to manage all fixed income sub-accounts.

    4. Employ an independent investment advisor to manage a certain group of sub-accounts and manage some sub-accounts internally.

Example: Employ Southeast Capital Management to manage all equity sub-accounts and manage all fixed-income accounts internally.

The asset management structure for managing sub-accounts' assets is not as important as the long-term investment results and record of consistency demonstrated by the financial advisor.

What is also important before an investor purchases an annuity is that he or she understands what sub-account investment alternatives are available, the investment objectives of each, the investment policies, and whether there are a sufficient number of investment alternatives available within a variable annuity sub-account structure to maintain an effective asset-allocation model.

Variable Annuity Separate and Sub-Accounts

An investor's next step in selecting appropriate sub-accounts for investing is understanding the relationship between the separate account and the sub-accounts.

A separate account (accumulation account) is a master investment account that acts as a conduit to the established accounts. All invested funds flow through the separate account into the various sub-accounts. Each sub-account has a specific investment objective. Combined with the other sub-accounts, this gives the investor the choice and the flexibility to select distinctly different portfolios to meet asset-allocation and diversification demands. (See Figure 4–1.)

An investor in a mutual fund purchases shares. An investor in a sub-account purchases accumulation units. Accumulation units are to variable annuities as fund shares are to mutual funds. Accumulation units (shares) are purchased by the contract owner at net asset value (NAV), without commissions, in full and fractional units. To compare, no-load mutual funds are also purchased at net asset value. Load funds that charge commissions are purchased from the net proceeds after deducting commissions.

Another difference is that, although it is not recommended, mutual fund shares certificates will be issued by the investment company if requested by the investor. Sub-account accumulation unit certificates are never issued.

Figure 4–1

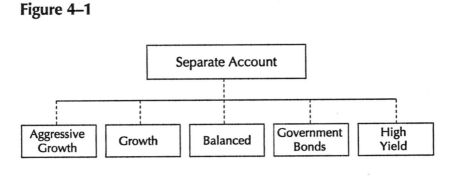

Determining Accumulation Unit Values

The net asset value of each accumulation unit (share) is determined at the close of trading of the New York Stock Exchange each day the Exchange is open. Accumulation unit values are determined each day by the insurance company or the financial advisor, as shown in Table 4–1.

This is extremely important and necessary because daily purchases and daily redemption prices are based on the NAV. Investors may learn the daily NAV (or closing price) by either calling the insurance company or consulting various financial publications.

Types of Sub-Accounts

Investor sub-account choices and numbers depend on the variable annuity contract, but sufficient flexibility exists with most variable annuities.

Understanding the investment objectives of each sub-account is critical in choosing an asset-allocation mix that matches the financial objectives and investment risk tolerance of an individual investor.

From a broad-brush investment overview, most investors seek a consistent, competitive return and the preservation of their capital.

Table 4–1. Determining Accumulation Unit Values

$$\frac{\text{Total Value of Sub-Account Assets} - \text{Liabilities}}{\text{Number of Outstanding Accumulation Units}} = \frac{\text{Net Asset Value}}{\text{per A/Unit}}$$

Example: $10,000,000 Net Value of Sub-Account
                 2,000,000 Accumulation Units Outstanding

$$\frac{\$10,000,000 \text{ Value}}{2,000,000 \text{ A/U}} = \$5.00 \text{ NAV per A/Unit}$$

While most investors understand the importance of financial security, few understand the nuances of financial planning and asset-allocation techniques. Even fewer investors understand or appreciate risk tolerance and the management of risk.

Sub-accounts may be divided into four broad categories:

1. Those seeking capital appreciation (stocks).
2. Those seeking fixed income (bonds).
3. Those combining stocks/bonds (balanced).
4. Those offering fixed-income money market rates.

Sub-Accounts Seeking Capital Appreciation

Aggressive Growth Sub-Account

This type seeks to provide investors with maximum capital appreciation (growth) by investing in aggressive, less seasoned growth stocks. Little consideration is given to receiving dividends, as receiving current income is not important. Diversification is gained through a stock portfolio of aggressive growth, emerging growth, and small capitalization company stocks.

During times of strong market advances, investors usually receive a better-than-average return on more aggressive investments. During market declines they usually experience worse-than-average losses.

Investing in this type of sub-account is not for the fainthearted. It is suitable only for sophisticated investors who maintain a well-diversified portfolio, understand the importance of a long-term investment strategy, understand risk and volatility, and can sustain investment losses that are often substantially higher than those experienced in a more conservative portfolio.

While aggressive growth investments produce higher risks, the news is not all disagreeable. The risks on these types of investments tend to dissipate over longer time periods, and aggressive growth sub-accounts usually produce highly competitive long-term results.

Investment Note: This type of investment is suitable only for investors with strong constitutions, long-term investment time frames, and aggressive attitudes. Aggressive growth sub-accounts should generally comprise only a small percentage of a total portfolio for even the most aggressive investor. Conservative investors should avoid them entirely.

Growth Sub-Accounts

This type seeks to provide investors with steady capital appreciation (asset growth) by investing in a diversified portfolio of well-seasoned and financially sound companies. The companies are usually included in the Standard & Poor's 500 and have demonstrated the ability to produce strong and consistent earnings, steady growth, and regular dividend payments. Dividends are often a secondary investment objective of this type of sub-account, as these companies have generally paid dividends over a long time period.

Because of the more consistent and less volatile long-term performance of these blue-chip investments, the portfolio's stocks have lower price/earnings ratios than aggressive stocks. A tolerance for moderate risk is still necessary to invest in solid growth stocks, but over the long term (more than 10 years) growth stocks have always outperformed other types of investments, especially bonds and CDs. This investment is suitable for investors seeking an above-average return from seasoned stocks and willing to accept reasonable long-term risk.

Investment Note: Conservative and seasoned growth stocks are the most appropriate long-term investments for meeting the challenges of inflation (that is, purchasing power). Growth stocks should always be a larger portion of a variable annuity's long-term asset-allocation model.

Growth and Income Sub-Account
(Equity Income Sub-Account)

This type seeks to provide investors with a competitive, long-term total return by investing in a portfolio that combines both equities (growth stocks) and fixed income (bonds). This investment strategy seeks to reduce risk and produce a more consistent and competitive return through the diversification of asset classes.

An equity income portfolio is conservative by its design and also places a high priority on the preservation of the sub-account's assets. The equities in the portfolio will usually be weighted toward well-seasoned stocks that pay above-average dividends. The portfolio usually also contains high-grade convertible bonds and fixed-income securities. An equity income portfolio is judged most successful when it produces consistent performance over the long term.

The most attractive feature of the growth and income sub-account is its consistent performance. It is the "Steady Eddie" approach to asset allocation: lower risk and consistent returns.

Investment Note: This investment is suitable for all conservative investors with a long-term investment horizon and the willingness to assume modest investment risk. Balanced, Total Return, Multistrategy, and Asset-Allocation sub-accounts are usually similar to Growth and Income sub-accounts, as most invest in a reasonably balanced combination of equities (common stocks) and corporate bonds. While similar, each type of sub-account will have its own approach to an asset-allocation model, the equity/income securities percentages, and the risk level assumed by the portfolio manager(s).

While an investor may be offered a number of equity sub-account alternatives, the primary choices are summarized in Table 4–2. Within the three equity sub-account classes are multiple choices that include foreign, global, sector, precious metals, small capitalization, emerging global and utility sub-accounts, among others. Most variable annuity sub-account investment alternatives will be

Table 4–2. Equity Sub-Account Alternatives

Class of Sub-Account	Risk	Investment Objective
Aggressive Growth	High	High Return
Growth	Moderate	Competitive
Balanced	Lower	Consistent

discussed in this chapter. However, it should be obvious that it is impossible for any variable annuity contract to offer an infinite array of investment choices, nor is it necessary. A good variable annuity contract should offer sufficient investment choices, not endless investment choices.

In our chapter on asset allocation, investors learn that they really have only three choices for sub-account investing: stocks, bonds, and cash. Accordingly, a clear understanding of fixed-income sub-accounts is our next goal in our quest for variable annuity investing success.

Investment Note: The appropriate initial investment decision is asset class (stocks and/or bonds); the *subsequent* choice is sub-accounts, not vice versa.

Fixed-Income Sub-Accounts

There are at least two investor types seeking to accumulate wealth: savers and investors. By definition an investor assumes risk and by tradition savers avoid risk, like a third cousin trying to borrow money. The most beautiful word in the language for a saver is "guaranteed."

Traditional fixed-income securities have two common features: a predetermined interest rate and a definite maturity date. This is true for all of the most common fixed-income securities, including corporate bonds, government securities, municipal bonds, foreign government and corporate bonds, and certificates of deposit (CDs).

Most fixed-income investments are considered conservative, secure, and predictable, particularly during periods of low inflation and steady or falling interest rates. They also offer the average investor "investment comfort" in the form of income stream certainty, purchaser familiarity, and perceived safety.

Certificates of Deposit

Of all fixed-income securities, the certificate of deposit remains the most popular. There are four major reasons for this support:

1. The guaranteed rate of return and return of principal.
2. Savers placing a disproportionate emphasis on the preservation of capital.
3. Savers lacking awareness and understanding of viable long-term investment alternatives.
4. Tradition. What was good enough for my parents is good enough for me.

Without question CDs and their guaranteed returns are appropriate for a portion of an investor's portfolio. Most financial advisors recommend CDs or money market funds to meet liquidity and emergency needs. That's the good news. The bad news is that CDs and money market funds are short-term saving vehicles, not long-term investment opportunities, and do not protect a saver against the erosion of buying power in a time of rising inflation. Hence, savers maintaining a high percentage of their assets in CDs should determine if the reallocation of a portion of those assets might be appropriate.

Investment Note: CDs are comfortable investments for savers but do not address inflation risk and the loss of purchasing power.

Bonds

Bonds, the second most common fixed-income asset group, also offer fixed rates of return and return of principal. However, unlike CDs, all bonds introduce the element of market and/or credit risk into the decision-making process. The hazard of credit risk is that the issuer will default on the interest and/or principal payments. The perils of market risk are that the market value of the bond will decrease as interest rates increase and/or credit risk concerns will arise.

Only U.S. government general obligation securities, backed by the full faith and credit of the U.S. government, and certain government agency securities are considered to be without credit risk. All fixed-income securities, including U.S. government bonds, are subject to market risk.

Further defined, there are three major classifications of fixed-income securities: government, corporate, and municipal bonds. Each offers a predictable and reliable income stream, and bonds tend to experience less market volatility than equities. The rate of return (yield) on fixed-income securities depends on three factors: the general interest rate environment, the creditworthiness of the bond, and the maturity of the bond.

Bonds offer both opportunities for capital gains and possibilities of capital losses. As interest rates fall, bonds prices rise. Conversely, as interest rates rise, bond prices fall. (See Table 4–3.)

Investment Note: As is the case when selecting equity sub-accounts, an investor need not be concerned about selecting specific

Table 4–3. Fixed Income Sub-Accounts

Sub-Accounts	Market Risk	Credit Risk	Investment Objective
U.S. Government	Yes	No	Income
U.S. Agencies	Yes	No	Income
Corporate Investment	Yes	Low	Income
Corporate High-Yield	Yes	Moderate	Income
Money Markets	No	Very Low	Income

fixed-income securities. Instead, the investor selects the sub-accounts that meet his or her investment objectives, risk tolerance, and asset-allocation requirements. No municipal bond sub-accounts are offered in variable annuity contracts because municipal bond interest is exempt from federal taxes.

U.S. Government Bond (Securities) Sub-Account

This type invests only in federal government securities, agencies, and instrumentalities. The sub-account's investment objective is to provide current income and safety of capital. The investments can include U.S. bills, notes, bonds, and STRIPs (zero coupons), and agencies such as GNMA, FHLMC, or FNMA. Many government bond sub-accounts include adjustable-rate instruments to reduce price volatility, as the rates are periodically reset to reflect current market conditions. Government bonds are without credit risk but are subject to market (price) risk, particularly in the longer maturities.

Investment Note: This investment is suitable for an investor seeking a stable income stream and lower price volatility. The sub-account's market risk level is moderate.

Types of U.S. Government Debt Securities

Treasury bills (T-bills): Short-term government obligations issued for 13-, 26-, and 52-week maturities. They are issued at a discount and mature at par. The minimum denomination issued is $10,000.

Treasury notes: Intermediate-term government obligations with maturities ranging from 2 to 10 years. They are issued at par and bear a specific rate of interest, which is paid every 6 months. They are sold in increments of $1,000.

Treasury bonds: Long-term government obligations with maturities ranging from 10 to 30 years. They are issued at par and bear a specific interest rate, which is paid every 6 months. They are issued in increments of $5,000.

The 30-year Treasury bond "long bond" rate is significant because it is a benchmark by which interest-rate fluctuations are measured and widely reported.

Zero coupon bonds: Long-term (usually) government obligations for which interest payments are not distributed to the bondholder until maturity. "Standard" zero coupon bonds are sold at a discount that reflects the yield and mature at par. For example:

$10,000, 10-year zero coupon priced to yield 8.0%
$10,000 × 0.46319 (present value) = $4,631.90

An investor pays $4,631.90 for the bond and receives $10,000 when it matures in 10 years.

Government National Mortgage Association (GNMA) bonds: "Ginnie Maes" are pools of mortgage securities guaranteed by the GNMA, which "passes-through" homeowners' interest and principal payments to investors. GNMA guarantees the performance of the mortgages.

Corporate Bond Sub-Accounts

Corporate bonds are debt instruments issued by corporations for building expansion, capital improvements, equipment purchases, or any number of other reasons corporations borrow money. Like most debt instruments, corporate bonds have a stated maturity date and pay a fixed rate of interest. Bonds often include other features such as conversion privileges, but are primarily purchased for their income stream.

A major consideration when purchasing corporate bonds is the issuer's creditworthiness. Blue-chip corporations seldom default on either interest or principal payments; thus, they are able to borrow capital at the most favorable prevailing rate. Conversely, lenders extract higher rates and impose stricter borrowing conditions on emerging companies and corporations with weaker balance sheets and shorter track records.

Corporate bonds issued by foreign corporations are subject to the same credit risk conditions as domestic corporations. Major foreign corporations borrow at more favorable rates, while emerging and less financially stable foreign corporations pay higher rates to borrow capital. However, there is an additional consideration when investing in foreign debt securities: currency exchange risk. Unless payment is required in U.S. dollars, currency fluctuations can increase leverage and exposure dramatically. Many sub-account managers "manage" this additional risk by extensive country diversification and/or currency hedging.

Investment-Grade Corporate Sub-Accounts

This type seeks current income, safety, and preservation of capital by investing in a portfolio of high-quality corporate bonds. Investment-grade securities are defined as securities that are rated investment grade (or comparable quality) by the various bond-rating services. Examples of investment-grade bond ratings are BBB or better by Standard & Poor's and Baa or better by Moody's.

Bonds with the highest credit rating (AAA) will pay the least interest on their fixed-income debt. As the quality of bonds decreases, interest rates increase. In a thriving economy, fixed-income money managers will often lower their average portfolio rating to receive additional yield. During less prosperous periods, money managers have a propensity toward raising their portfolio's quality rating.

Sub-account managers have an array of choices when purchasing investment-grade corporate bonds. All major U.S. and foreign corporations issue debt securities. Creditworthiness is the money manager's first consideration when selecting; the second is maturity. Bonds are issued with varying maturity dates but are categorized as short-, intermediate-, and long term. The importance of maturity cannot be overemphasized. Except in unusual market circumstances (inverted yield curve), bonds with longer maturities pay higher interest rates and carry more market risk.

To lower market risk, fixed-income sub-account managers diversify their portfolios by purchasing bonds with varying maturity dates. (See Table 4–4.)

Investment Note: There is a direct correlation between a bond's price volatility and its maturity date.

Investment-grade bond sub-accounts are suitable for investors seeking quality fixed-income investments, a reliable income stream, and moderate volatility. The sub-account credit risk level is low. The interest rate risk is moderate.

High-Yield Bond Sub-Accounts

The question arises why anyone would want to invest in "junk bonds." The much maligned high-yield bond market offers the discerning and knowledgeable investor an opportunity for very competitive yields and capital appreciation. It offers the less sophisticated investor an opportunity for disaster.

Table 4–4. Bond Maturity Definitions

Short Term-Maturity	2 Years or Less
Intermediate-Term Maturity	2 to 10 Years
Long-Term Maturity	10 to 30 Years

High-yield bonds are called "junk" bonds because of their lower ratings and additional risk of default. As with any risk/reward scenario, the opportunity for highly competitive yields is counterbalanced by an exposure to higher credit risks and higher default rates compared to investment-grade bonds.

High-yield bonds can be subject to substantial price erosion during slow economic times or when questions arise about a bond issuer's creditworthiness. Their volatility is usually substantially higher than that of investment-grade bonds.

An individual investor is best served by not purchasing individual high-yield bonds, EVER. The high-yield bond market is too sophisticated and should be left to the professionals. However, it does not preclude an individual investor's participation in this sometimes highly rewarding market by purchasing high yield bond mutual funds.

As with aggressive growth stocks, high-yield bonds can have a positive effect and reduce risk through diversification. The question is not return, but risk exposure. Most investors are comfortable with a moderate percentage of high-yield bonds in their sub-account asset-allocation model.

Investment Note: Like good food and drink, high-yield bond funds are great in moderation, but overindulgence could create problems.

High-yield bond funds are suitable only for sophisticated investors seeking higher returns and possible capital appreciation from speculative fixed-income instruments. The fund risk is high; these funds should never be more than a small percentage of one's total investments.

Money Market Sub-Accounts

There is only one reason a variable annuity investor should have assets in a money market fund: to temporarily "park" the money until a long-term equity or bond sub-account investment decision is made. Variable annuity money market sub-accounts are extremely useful and appropriate for short-term investing, but variable annuities are long-term investment vehicles.

Asset allocation models include three groups: stocks, bonds, and cash. Money markets meet the "cash" requirement by seeking short-term competitive returns and safety through a portfolio of short-term money market instruments such as CDs, Treasury bills, and highest quality commercial paper. Money markets are not suitable investment vehicles for long-term investing in variable annuities. They should be used as transitional vehicles for investors either seeking a safe haven during times of market uncertainty or waiting for an appropriate investment opportunity.

The major categories of variable annuity sub-accounts available for investors are shown in Table 4–5.

Special Situation Sub-Accounts

Most variable annuity investors allocate their assets among the major sub-account investment categories. However, many variable annuity

Table 4–5. Variable Annuity Sub-Accounts

Sub-Account	Investments	Primary Objective	Credit Risk	Market Risk
Aggressive Growth	Stocks	Growth	N/A	Highest
Growth	Stocks	Growth	N/A	High
Balanced	Stocks/Bonds	Combined	Low	Lower
Government Bonds	Bonds	Income	None	Medium
Investment-Grade Bonds	Bonds	Income	Lower	Medium
High-Yield Bonds	Bonds	Income	High	Highest
Money Market	Cash Equivalent	Income	Lowest	Lowest
Special Situation	Varies	Varies	Varies	Varies

contracts have expanded their options to include additional choices from the most aggressive to the most conservative equity and fixed-income investments. It is not possible to include all sub-accounts available, but some of the more common are described below.

International Equity and Global Sub-Accounts

International sub-accounts invest for capital appreciation through a portfolio invested in foreign equity securities of the companies whose primary operations are outside the United States. (Global sub-accounts include U.S. securities.)

Usually an international equity sub-account will diversify with securities from a number of foreign countries. Foreign markets have grown to represent over two-thirds of the world's capitalization and annualized returns during the past 10 years. Funds are available for specific countries or specific regions. The areas that dominate world stock funds are the United States, Japan, Europe, and the Pacific Rim. Investing in foreign securities requires sophisticated and specialized knowledge. Returns are affected not only by a foreign company's earnings but also by currency transactions and the local political environment.

This investment is suitable only for sophisticated investors willing to assume a higher degree of risk. The opportunities for above-average returns are substantial but are counterbalanced by the additional market and currency risks.

Investment Note: Investors should consider investing a portion of their assets in foreign equity securities for both diversification and highly competitive growth opportunities.

International (Foreign) Bond Sub-Accounts

International bond sub-accounts are the fixed-income equivalent of their foreign equity companions. These sub-accounts seek high current income, safety, and preservation of capital by investing in a portfolio of foreign fixed-income securities. (Global sub-accounts include U.S. fixed income securities.)

Because of their real or perceived higher risk, foreign bond sub-accounts generally offer higher yields. Like other foreign securities, these sub-accounts are subject to market risk, currency exchange risk and, depending on the portfolio mix, varying degrees of credit risk.

This investment is suitable only for sophisticated investors who are seeking higher fixed returns and who understand that foreign bond funds are subject to more volatility than domestic bond funds. Conversely, this type of sub-account's return potential is also greater.

Sector Equity Sub-Accounts

Many variable annuity contracts offer the opportunity to invest in a particular segment of the economy, such as the airline, chemical, automotive, paper, or banking industries. This microinvestment approach adversely affects the risk-reward investment scenario significantly because of the lack of diversification. The purpose of hiring professional money managers and diversifying investment assets is to increase the opportunity for more consistent and competitive long-term investment results. Sector sub-accounts are counterproductive to that investment objective.

Like aggressive growth and high-yield sub-accounts, this type of sub-account is suitable for a small portion of an aggressive equity portfolio. Conservative investors are better served by less volatile and more diversified sub-accounts.

Small Capitalization Equity Sub-Accounts

These sub-accounts are quite similar to most aggressive growth sub-accounts. They seek an above-average return by investing in stocks of newly emerging or smaller-capitalized companies. Often a limitation on the size of the capitalization of the company is included in the investment selection process; for instance, only companies with a total capitalization of $500,000,000 or less qualify. They experience higher volatility than other equity sub-accounts.

Utility Stock Sub-Accounts

While technically an equity investment, utility sub-accounts are more similar to fixed-income sub-accounts. Their objectives are to provide a competitive dividend yield through the purchase of the stocks of major utilities, preserve capital assets, and experience modest capital appreciation. While utilities provide only modest asset growth, these sub-accounts can offer attractive total returns and can be particularly attractive investments during times of market uncertainty and declining interest rates.

Utility sub-accounts are well suited for conservative investors seeking a safe haven during times of market uncertainty.

Precious Metals Sub-Accounts

Precious metals sub-accounts are the modern-day answer to traditional gold mutual funds. Until the late 1970s many investment advisors recommended a percentage allocation to gold funds to offset inflation. The concept has been expanded to include other precious metals stocks and the actual commodity.

Precious metals sub-accounts seek aggressive capital appreciation by investing in precious metals and mining stocks throughout the world. These funds are the most speculative sub-account available in most variable annuity contracts. They are highly specialized and are usually considered sector sub-accounts.

These sub-accounts experience diminishing support during periods of relatively low inflation rates and stable commodity prices, and they offer investment alternatives.

Precious metals are suitable investments during times of high inflation and troubling world events. Surprisingly, despite the potential volatility, the inclusion of precious metals funds in an asset-allocation model can reduce portfolio risk and volatility. However, con-

servative investors are generally better served by a less speculative
approach to asset management.

Summary

- Understanding the investment objectives, diversification
  strategies, and relative risks of a variable annuity's sub-
  accounts allows an investor to make knowledgeable asset-
  allocation decisions.
- There are three major asset-allocation investment categories
  from which to choose: stocks, bonds, and cash.
- An annuity investor is only responsible for choosing the
  combination of sub-accounts that meet his or her long-term
  investment objectives. The asset manager is responsible for
  selecting the individual portfolio securities.
- Sub-account diversification is essential for competitive
  and consistent long-term asset growth. An investor can
  design a portfolio from seven major categories and other
  special situations.
- There is always a direct correlation between a sub-account's
  potential return and its potential risk. The higher the risk,
  the higher the reward potential, and vice versa.
- Money market sub-accounts are appropriate and necessary for
  asset allocation and for the safety essential during market
  uncertainty. However, money markets are short-term investment vehicles and are not appropriate for meeting a variable
  annuity's goal of long-term competitive and consistent
  growth.
- Conservative investors are best served by allocating assets to
  sub-accounts that have demonstrated consistent growth and
  are well diversified. Substantial exposure to aggressive
  growth, high-yield, and sector sub-accounts is most often
  not appropriate.

5

RETIREMENT PLANNING

Investment Flexibility

Annuities offer investors many options to meet investment objectives. Both the financial goals of funding retirement and accumulating wealth are particularly well served by using annuities. The ability to compound growth tax-deferred is an essential element. Variable annuity sub-accounts further enhance long-term investment opportunities through choice and diversification. Annuities can meet the investment objectives of both affluent investors seeking tax deferral and long-term wealth accumulation and average investors seeking a more competitive investment vehicle to fund their retirement needs.

To meet the financial needs of investors it is important to understand their investment strategy and demographics. Most potential and participating annuity investors are mature (50+), conservative savers, not investors. Investors, by definition, willingly assume calculated risk.

From an investment perspective, nonannuity investors are comfortable with guaranteed returns and the guaranteed return of principal. They have little understanding of inflation-induced purchasing power loss or the benefits of tax-deferred wealth accumulation. They often use short-term investment strategies (such as CDs) to address long-term financial goals and objectives.

Annuity purchasers (and most investors) have at least four major investment concerns:

1. Adequate monthly retirement income.
2. Market risk on their investments.
3. Depletion of assets for retirement living expenses.
4. Liquidity for major medical and other emergencies.

Addressing investor concerns requires planning, persistence, and professional guidance. Successful investors most often direct their investments into broad areas (diversification), with annuities as one part of their long-term financial plan.

Should a variable annuity be included in a retirement portfolio? For long-term investors the short answer is probably yes. Annuities are excellent vehicles for funding retirement, particularly when combined with qualified retirement plans. For example, retirement plans require the commencement of distributions when the owner reaches 70 1/2. Annuities have no such statutory requirement. Distributions can be postponed indefinitely, the value continues to grow tax-deferred, and none of the deferred income is included in Social Security income inclusion calculations.

An Overview of Financial Planning with Variable Annuities

The goal of most investors is reaching financial independence within an acceptable risk-reward framework that includes an acceptable time period. To accomplish this goal an investor should remember that annuities can be a major contributor to success. However, most investors will require a balanced and diversified group of assets to reach their objectives. This is particularly true for affluent investors seeking wealth accumulation in addition to funding retirement.

Wealth accumulation and retirement planning require three steps: establishing goals and objectives, implementing a long-term investment plan, and periodically monitoring and evaluating the results. Also, the need to accumulate wealth to fund an individual's future has never been greater.

Unlike recent employment eras in which productive, loyal employees were reasonably assured of job security, medical benefits, and retirement pensions, the majority of today's employees are concerned about job security, current and future financial stability, rising medical costs, and funding retirement and college education.

In less than 20 years, the burden of individual financial security, particularly retirement funding, has dramatically shifted from corporate employers to individual employees. Contributing to this reallocation of responsibility are corporate downsizings, recessions, mergers, and fierce domestic and foreign competition. The causes are less important than the stark reality that most individuals are now more directly responsible for funding their own financial needs. Like trying to pay a $50.00 dinner check and with a $20.00 bill, the problem is clearly defined: the solution requires more thought. Most investors understand that accumulating wealth is difficult. The solution is developing a long-term financial plan to reach specific investment goals.

Few investors have developed a definitive investment strategy or the investment sophistication to implement strategies such as asset allocation, risk management, and diversification to reach their goals. The situation is further exacerbated by conservative investors, who, through tradition, lack of investment knowledge, and fear of risk, place a disproportionate importance on the preservation of capital and guaranteed returns while ignoring the indisputable risk of inflation (lost of purchasing power). This approach satisfies a saver's emotional goal of risk avoidance but does not meet the investment objective of all successful investors: receiving a competitive and consistent return within the constraints of acceptable risk in order to receive a positive net return.

Designing and implementing an appropriate financial plan is not difficult. Like planning a trip, one determines the destination, type of transportation, travel time required, and the method of payment. In investment terms, this translates as:

Financial Goals + Types of Investments + Time Line +
Funding Methods = Financial Planning

Developing a long-term financial plan is like following the road map for your trip; you can't decide how to get where you are going until you understand where you are. That means you should determine the following information before you make any significant financial planning decisions.

The 11-Point Financial Planning Checklist

1. What are my present and future investment goals?
2. What is my net worth?

3. What are my present and future income expectations?
4. What is my time line for meeting my investment goals?
5. What is my tolerance for risk?
6. How will my financial plan be funded?
7. Should investment advisor(s) join my team?
8. What are my current expenses and spending habits?
9. What will be my income requirements for retirement?
10. Are my legal affairs in order?
11. Are there special circumstances to consider?

A Systematic Approach to Meeting Financial Goals

Few investors have the expertise to manage their personal assets in a manner that maximizes their return for the level of risk taken. This lack of knowledge, combined with another hindrance to wealth accumulation, procrastination, creates an atmosphere in which investors are usually doomed to mediocrity or, worse, outright failure.

To reiterate, the approach to successful investing is straightforward. The building blocks are knowledge, discipline, consistency, and time horizon. The capstone is realistic expectations:

Knowledge + Discipline + Consistency + Time Horizon + Realistic Expectations = Successful Investment Results

Knowledge gives an investor the ability to clearly define his or her specific financial goals and objectives. Discipline demands that the investor continue with the program during both prosperous and difficult times. Consistency requires that the investor make regular contributions, diversify assets, and monitor the results. Time is also critical to financial planning. As the time horizon expands, investment contribution demands decrease. The "magic of compounding" benefits exponentially from expanding time horizons. Long-term risk is reduced. Investment returns are more consistent.

The capstone of successful investing is realistic expectations. There is no free lunch. The saver assuming no risk and purchasing certificates of deposit is guaranteed a rate of return and the return of principal. The counterbalance for total principal safety and guaranteed fixed returns is the erosion of purchasing power and the lost opportunity for capital appreciation.

The investor accepting a degree of risk anticipates a higher return. When successful, competitive returns are the result. Again, there is no free lunch. The counterbalance for assuming an acceptable degree of risk is the potential loss of investment capital. The higher the return opportunity, the higher the risk exposure.

Unsophisticated investors often have unrealistic investment return expectations. In these cases the investor has the obligation to become more educated about the relationship between risk and reward. As part of a conservative, long-term strategy, realistic investment return expectations should be determined prior to committing assets. Sophisticated investors and financial advisors measure long-term performance over a horizon (market cycle) of at least three to five years. Ten years is an even better time period, as it substantially increases the opportunity for consistent and competitive returns while also reducing short-term market risk.

Defining an investor's financial goal(s) aids in the design of an appropriate investment program. Traditional financial goals for investors include:

1. Funding retirement.
2. Funding educational expenses.
3. Receiving competitive investment returns.
4. Preserving capital.
5. Maintaining asset liquidity for emergencies.

Of all investment goals, retirement and college funding are the most common. In seeking those goals, investors are most comfortable with programs that are conservative, consistent, traditional, and limited in risk.

The opportunity to reach an investor's ultimate goal(s) can be enhanced by combining short-term and long-term objectives. The money saved from eliminating credit-card debt and its high interest charges can be invested in a mutual fund or an annuity. The money saved by extending the useful life of an automobile by 18 months through proper maintenance, thereby eliminating 18 car payments, can be significant enough to fully fund an IRA.

The benefit of planning and saving even small amounts cannot be overemphasized. Table 5–1 presents investors with a systematic approach to identifying both short- and long-term investment objectives, establishing a specific time period to meet those objectives, and determining their relative importance. Obviously each individual's short- and long-term goals are different, and priorities will change

Table 5–1. An Outline for Establishing Financial Goals

Importance	Time Period	Short-Term Goals
Eliminating Credit-Card Debt	1	6 months
Home Down Payment	1	18 months
Furnishing Home	3	24 months
Vacation	5	12 months
Car (pay cash)	2	24 months
Other		Varies
Long-Term Goals		
Funding Retirement	1	25 years
Funding Education	1	10 years
Remodeling Home	3	4 years
Purchasing Vacation Home	5	12 years
Purchasing Sailboat	4	4 years
Scale:	1 = Most Important	5 = Least Important

over time. Nevertheless, Table 5–1 provides a systematic and visual approach to establishing priorities and establishing financial goals.

Investment Note: The most important information in financial planning is identifying your investment objective.

An Investor's Net Worth

You can utilize all the strategies, buy/sell programs, charts, graphs, and economic theories you desire, but the bottom line remains: to build wealth, you must take in more than you put out.

Determining personal net worth is another easy but important step in an investor's quest for financial independence. This step provides information on an investor's current financial status, asset allocation mix, funds available for investment, and reallocation needs. Table 5–2 will help investors formulate a personal "balance sheet."

Once you have determined your net worth, it should be more apparent if your current allocation of assets is addressing your investment objectives. It should also be discernible if an asset reallocation is necessary and/or what liquid assets are more appropriately invested long-term.

The next step in financial planning is to determine monthly income and expenses. By monitoring receipts and disbursements, investors can analyze their income sources and determine their spending and saving patterns. This analysis assists investors in identifying opportunities for the reallocation of resources to meet investment objectives. Table 5–3 provides a cash-flow worksheet.

The Importance of Time

You have determined your financial goals, net worth, income sources, expenditures, and assets available for investing. The final ingredient of the investment planning equation is time. Time is important to investing for at least four reasons. As the time horizon expands:

1. Capital contribution requirements are reduced.
2. Long-term investment risk is reduced.

Table 5–2. Personal Balance Sheet Formula
Assets – Liabilities = Net Worth

Assets	
Assets	
Liquid (Cash Equivalent) Assets	
Checking Account	
Money Market Account	
Savings Account(s)	
Total Liquid Assets	
Liquid Investment Assets	
Stocks	
Bonds	
Mutual Funds	
Annuities	
Life Insurance Cash Value	
Certificates of Deposit	
Total Investment Assets	
Long-Term Retirement Assets	
401(k) plan	
IRA	
Other Retirement Plans	
Long-Term Investment Assets	
Current Market Value Home	
Investment Real Estate Equity	
Trusts	
Business Ownership Equity	
Collections (Net Sale Value)	
Other	
Total Long-Term Assets	
Other Assets	
Automobiles	
Liabilities	
Current Liabilities	
Credit Card Balances	
Bank and Credit Union Loans	
Automobile/Equipment Loans	
Other	
Other	
Other	
Total Current Liabilities	
Long-Term Liabilities	
Home Mortgage	
Investment Property Mortgage	
Other	
Total Long-Term Liabilities	
Net Worth (Assets – Liabilities)	

3. The dynamics of compounding become more dramatic.

4. Investment procrastination grows more costly.

Distinctly different attitudes exist between investors of varying ages. A younger investor's perception of his or her financial planning needs, particularly retirement planning, will differ from that of a more mature investor. Yet, all investors recognize the necessity of wealth accumulation. At any age, investing, especially on a tax-deferred basis, is a critical ingredient for financial security. Small investments made at an early age will grow substantially. The "magic" of compounding is never more evident than when investments are allowed to accumulate and grow for an extended period of time.

Individuals have many excuses for not investing. They are saving for a home, funding a college education, or they "will never retire" because they enjoy working. The solution for persuading investors to end their wealth accumulation and retirement planning procrastination and to immediately begin investing is through education and knowledge. Here are some critical reasons to start an investment program *immediately:*

- Retirement planning responsibility is now with the individual, not corporate America and the government.
- All the money invested benefits the investor and his/her family.
- The tax incentives for investing in annuities, tax-free bonds, retirement plans, and other tax-deferred vehicles are immense.
- Most retirees need 70% to 80% of their preretirement income to maintain their standard of living.
- Procrastination is expensive. Every six-year delay will double an investor's future cost. (Rule of 72 at 12%)
- With 5% inflation, the cost of goods and services doubles every 15 years.
- Accumulating wealth brings financial independence.

Table 5–3. Cash Flow Analysis

Monthly Income	
Employment Income (Net)	
Social Security Income	
Investment Income	
Certificates of Deposit	
Rental Property	
Other	
Total Current Income	
Monthly Fixed Expenses	
Home Mortgage	
Home Insurance and Property Taxes	
Automobile Payment	
Monthly Investment Plans	
Insurance	
Medical Insurance	
Club Dues	
Other Fixed Expenses	
Total Monthly Expenses	
Monthly Variable Expenses	
Food	
Utilities	
Transportation	
Entertainment	
Other Variable Expenses	
Total Variable Expenses	
Surplus (Deficit) Monthly Cash Flow	
Allocation of Surplus Funds	
Savings Account	
Investments	
Checking Account	

The Cost of Procrastination

You can see from Table 5–4 that the annual investment required to become a millionaire at age 65 increases considerably as the number of years remaining before one reaches the age of 65 decreases.

Risk Tolerance

Understanding the relationship between risk and reward is extremely important for all investors and it is discussed in greater depth in the chapter on asset allocation. The most important fact to remember is that the loss of purchasing power (inflation) is a much bigger risk than the loss of capital from long-term equity and bond investing. When asset class and security diversification are added to the equation, risk is further reduced and consist performance and competitive return opportunities also increase.

Table 5–4. Becoming a Millionaire at Age 65 Through Annual Investments, Assuming a 10% Tax-Deferred Rate of Return

Age	Years to Retirement	Annual Contribution
25	40	$2,259
30	35	3,690
35	30	6,079
40	25	10,168
45	20	17,460
50	15	31,474
55	10	62,745
60	5	163,797

Using Professional Advisors for Retirement Planning

The most important element in an investor's choice of a financial advisor is trust. An investor must be comfortable with the representative or the relationship will not grow or prosper. Conversely, the advisor must also feel that he or she has the confidence of the investor in order to implement the appropriate investment strategies.

Unless a financial advisor has an existing and satisfactory relationship, building trust with an investor requires both time and effort. The advisor must display honesty, integrity, investment expertise, product knowledge, and a clear, compassionate understanding of the investor's goals, objectives, emotions, and concerns.

As a practical matter, an investor is well served using an advisor for financial planning and/or purchasing investments, particularly annuities. Annuities are highly specialized and sometimes complex investments whose features and benefits should be fully understood before purchase.

It is recommended that investors interview several financial advisors before making a final selection. When selecting a financial advisor there are a number of questions that should be answered. Legitimate and experienced advisors are always willing to answer them. It is important for an investor to feel comfortable before making any commitment. The most important question to ask a financial advisor is how he or she will contribute to the investor's wealth-accumulation and retirement plan. Other questions that should be asked include:

1. What is the advisor's experience? Is he or she experienced and knowledgeable about investments and financial planning?
2. What are the advisor's academic and industry credentials? What licenses and designations does he or she hold?
3. What bank, brokerage, insurance, or financial planning firm does he or she represent? What is the reputation of the institution?

4. Has the advisor had numerous customer complaints or has he or she been sanctioned by regulatory agencies for inappropriate behavior?
5. Does the advisor offer a complete array of products and services, including mutual funds, annuities, insurance, and other investment opportunities to meet diversification and asset allocation needs?
6. What is the advisor's approach to long-term investing?
7. Will the advisor be available for service and counsel after the sale?
8. What type of clientele does the advisor service? Does he or she understand the needs of your demographic group?
9. How is the advisor compensated? By commissions or charge fees, or a combination of both?
10. Are customer and trade references available?

The Importance of Risk in Retirement Planning

This book has previously emphasized and will continue to emphasize that the biggest risk long-term investors face is the loss of purchasing power through inflation, not market risk.

Accepting risk is not unusual. It is part of our daily lives. From the proverbial taking a chance crossing the street to skydiving, a degree of risk always exists. Defining investment risk is another matter. It is subjective and highly personal, but the definition of investing includes accepting risk.

The real questions are: What is your investor profile? and What degree of risk are you willing to accept? The answer lies in a number of considerations including your age, retirement needs, anticipated retirement date, and comfort level with market fluctuations.

Most advisors recommend reducing risk as a retirement date grows closer. However, they also most often recommend that regardless of age, a portion of all investments remain in equities to offset inflation. Risk and return is discussed at length in the chapter on asset allocation.

Estate Planning

Estate planning is simply making the decisions on how you want your assets distributed upon your death. A will details your decisions and it is critical that your will be legal and current. Estate planning should also include a strategy for minimizing or eliminating estate taxes. For larger estates, marital and charitable deductions, lifetime transfers, and annual gifts may be appropriate. For estates under $600,000 estate taxes may be entirely eliminated.

Estate planning might also include a revocable living trust. While this type of trust does not offer income-tax savings or estate-tax advantages, it can be designed to meet most estate planning objectives. These trusts can consolidate your estate, have its assets professionally managed, and be administered by a trustee should the grantor be incapacitated in any manner.

Is it an appropriate vehicle for an investor? That should only be determined after consulting with an estate attorney and/or CPA or other competent counsel. However, the point is that estate planning is another element of successful financial planning.

How Much Money Will Be Needed at Retirement?

As a general rule, financial advisors feel that it requires 80% of a retiree's prior income to maintain his or her standard of living. For example, an investor with a present net annual income of $50,000 per year will need $40,000 ($50,000 × 80%) annually to maintain his or her preretirement living standard. Sources for funding this retirement are detailed in Table 5–5. In this case the idividual must determine how to fund a shortfall of $8,000 per year. This investor, assuming an 8% annual return from equities, will need an additional $100,000 ($100,000 × 8% = $8,000) to fund his or her retirement.

Caveat: Retirement needs are determined in current dollar values. The needs calculation should be adjusted annually to reflect inflation and purchasing power erosion.

Ten Misconceptions About Retirement and Retirement Planning

It is impossible to discuss all the nuances of retirement planning in a single chapter, or a single text, for that matter. However, there are at least ten major factors that should be understood by every investor planning for retirement.

1   A retiree's major goal should be the preservation of capital to assure security during retirement.

Table 5–5. Funding Annual Retirement Income

Social Security Benefits	$18,000
Company Retirement Program	5,000
IRA Income	2,000
Annuities	3,000
Mutual Funds	3,000
Certificates of Deposit	1,000
Projected Retirement Income	32,000
Projected Total Annual Income Needed	40,000
Additional Income Needed	8,000

Although preservation of capital is important, a retiree's biggest risk is loss of purchasing power (inflation), not market risk.

2. During retirement my health insurance will be provided by my employer and the government.

Rapidly rising medical insurance premiums caused by spiraling medical costs have forced most major employers to sharply reduce or eliminate medical coverage for their retired employees. This, coupled with increased demands on our Medicare system, have made self-funded medical care a reality.

3. Social Security will fund my retirement.

Social Security is the major source of income for a majority of retirees. Because of this, unfortunately, the majority of retirees lack sufficient retirement income to live comfortably. To retire in dignity it is imperative that retirees have additional income and assets.

4. When we "pay off" the car we will start saving. (Or any one of the 101 other excuses available.)

Procrastination is a real wealth-killer. Shorter investment time periods require larger contributions, increase risk, and make achieving financial goals less likely. It is very important to start investing today.

5. Owning your own home sharply reduces living expenses.

Many retirees who own their homes are now paying more in annual property taxes than their original annual mortgage payments. While the mortgage has been eliminated, property taxes, maintenance costs, and utility expenses continue to escalate.

6. My taxes will be greatly reduced during retirement.

In actual dollars that is often true, but investors still pay federal and state taxes in addition to taxes on their homes, automobiles, investments, capital gains, property, Social Security benefits, and anything else that comes to the attention of our state and federal governments.

7. We will travel and enjoy life once the children are gone.

You could be waiting a long time for that dream trip to Bora Bora. Children are leaving home later and many are returning as higher living costs and job scarcity make independent living less of an option for younger adults.

8. I will always have a good income as I am never going to retire.

Older and more experienced employees demand more compensation and make more demands on their health insurance. In addition, more companies are downsizing and streamlining, euphemistic terms for eliminating high-compensation positions filled by senior employees.

9. I really don't need much retirement savings. I will only live 5 to 10 years after retiring at 65.

Individuals reaching the retirement age of 65 have a life expectancy of 86 or older. With the quality of geriatric medicine continually improving, these longevity numbers will only increase (see Table 5–6).

10. We have some family money for retirement.

Hopefully you are correct. However, as our population ages, more parents are looking to their children for financial support rather than the reverse. Individuals are sometimes responsible for the financial well-being of both their children and their parents. This so-called barbell effect can be devastating to retirement planning and wealth accumulation.

Table 5–6. Life Expectancy

Female		Male	
Current Age	**Life Expectancy**	**Current Age**	**Life Expectancy**
60	26	60	23
65	22	65	19
70	18	70	15
75	14	75	12
80	11	80	9

Source: IRS (Publication 590) Life Expectancy Tables

Summary

- Variable annuities are outstanding investments for meeting long-term investment objectives, including wealth accumulation and funding retirement.
- Increasingly, individuals are responsible for funding their own retirement and other financial needs. Competition and economic realities dictate that corporations are no longer willing to generously fund retirement and medical benefits for retirees.
- Most investors lack the knowledge to effectively manage their assets.
- The four elements of successful investing are knowledge, discipline, consistency, and time. These must be combined with realistic expectations to meet retirement and wealth-accumulation expectations.

- Investors have five primary investment objectives: funding retirement, funding education, competitive investment returns, preservation of capital, and maintaining emergency funds.
- The initial step in financial planning is determining an individual's net worth. The next step is determining personal cash flow.
- Accepting risk as a part of systematic and diversified investing is often difficult for savers. Losing capital is an identifiable reality; receiving an above-average return is a subjective thesis.
- Using financial advisors in financial planning is usually a good idea for investors. Their expertise and guidance can make the difference in an investor's quest for financial independence.
- Financial planning includes estate planning and determining the amount of assets and income necessary to retire in comfort.
- There are at least 10 major misconceptions regarding retirement planning. Gaining the truth is essential to successful financial planning.

6

RETIREMENT PLANS

KEY CONCEPTS

▼ Qualified Retirement Plans Are the
#1 Tax Shelter Available

▼ Defined Benefit Plans

▼ Defined Contribution Plans

▼ Maximizing Retirement Plan Contributions

The purchase of an annuity is not an isolated occurrence. As we have learned, combining variable and fixed annuities with qualified retirement plans, tax-free bonds, mutual funds, and other growth and fixed-income investments creates a more diversified, synergistic, and effective investment strategy than the isolated purchase of a specific investment.

There are a number of qualified investment plans available to employers and employees. The Federal Tax Code offers a powerful incentive for employers to establish and for employees to participate in retirement plans: tax deferral. Even so, 47% of all U.S. households are not covered by a qualified pension plan.*

As an investment advisor, my recommendation is that working individuals eligible to contribute to a qualified retirement plan make their maximum allowable annual contribution unless there are mitigating circumstances. The logic behind this recommendation is simple. Investing in a qualified retirement plan is a great deal! As an employee contributing to a 401(k) or similar qualified retirement plan, you receive special tax advantages. This includes excluding your contributions from current taxation and building retirement assets with tax-deferred growth. Employer contributions to your account are also not included in your current income.

Qualified retirement plans can be complex, but all share some common features. All plans are established by an employer. All contributions are removed from the direct control of the employer to a trustee. The plan is a formal document with specific rules and regulations. Everyone who meets the eligibility requirements must be allowed to participate if they so choose.

Presenting the requirements of plan design, qualification standards, participation formulas, distribution rules, and the other multifarious decrees of certain plans is beyond the intent or scope of this book. Our focus remains on how to maximize your investment returns, reduce your risk, and build your wealth. If we discover some tax advantages for you along the way, so much the better. However, it is important that you understand the relationship between variable annuities and qualified retirement plans and their potential for your investment planning efforts.

Whether you are a financial advisor, company owner, employee, or soon-to-be retiree, understanding that qualified retirement plans can be major contributors to financial security is essential.

---

* Source: Buck Consultants, estimate.

It is meaningful to know why an employer sponsors a plan. It is as important to know why employees should participate. It is particularly important for the soon-to-be retiree types to answer such questions as, "Now that I have all this money for retirement, what do I do with it?"

The type of plan adopted depends on an employer's operation, motivation, and ability to fund the plan. Qualified retirement plans can be sponsored by a sole proprietorship, partnership, or corporation of any size. Whoever the sponsor, the single overriding objective is to provide for the retirement of the plan's participant(s). Sole proprietorships and small partnership groups generally adopt qualified plans that are less complex to administer, such as Individual Retirement Accounts (IRAs), Keogh Plans, and Simplified Employee Pension Plans (SEPs). Larger groups usually offer employees more flexible plans, such as 401(k)s. Again, regardless of the qualified plan type, contributions are deductible and earnings accumulate tax-deferred.

A sole proprietorship's motive for contributing to a qualified plan is straightforward. The participant funds his or her retirement, deducts the contributions, reduces federal income tax obligations, and keeps all the money in a personal retirement account. Nice work if you can get it.

Partnerships and small corporations share basically the same motivations.

Large corporations often have a more complex agenda. In addition to the aforementioned tax savings and other major benefits, larger companies are able to recruit and retain higher quality, loyal employees with generously funded qualified retirement plans.

Qualified Plans

A qualified plan is an employee benefit that qualifies for favorable tax treatment by the Internal Revenue Service (IRS). The basic translation: if the plan is for the exclusive benefit of the employees and the sponsor adheres to the rules and regulations, the plan participants receive tax-deferred accumulation and other benefits allowed by the Internal Revenue Code.

Qualified plans are classified as either defined benefit or defined contribution plans. As one might imagine, a defined benefit plan promises a specific retirement benefit(s) to the participant(s).

A defined contribution plan's value and eventual benefits depend on the total contributions and the overall performance of the underlying assets. These two plan types are analogous to variable and fixed annuities. One plan's benefits are guaranteed (like a fixed annuity) while the other plan's benefits depend on performance (like a variable annuity).

Of the two groups, defined contribution plans are the most common. In these plans participants are not guaranteed specific benefits. Individual accounts are established to record the amount of each participant's earned benefits. The assets are distributed to the participants at retirement.

Many employers prefer defined contribution plans because of their flexibility. A good illustration is a profit-sharing plan, a form of defined contribution plan. An employer's profit-sharing plan contribution can be fully discretionary. A company with an erratic earnings history or a relatively new company might find this feature particularly attractive. Established or larger companies with profit-sharing plans often establish a formula to contribute a certain percentage of each employee's earnings to their individual account. Say an employee earns $40,000 annually and the company contributes 5% of the employee's earnings to his or her profit-sharing retirement account ($2,000).

Defined contribution plan assets can be more aggressively invested than defined benefit plans. Since the retirement benefits are not guaranteed, the assets can be diversified into other investments including individual stocks and bonds, mutual funds, or insurance products.

However, investment flexibility does not relieve plan sponsors of their fiduciary responsibilities. Employers managing their plan's assets must manage prudently, including diversification to reduce risk. Sponsors requiring participants to allocate their own assets must still provide sufficient, suitable, and judicious investment choices.

Investment Note: Under Section 404(c) of ERISA, fiduciary responsibilities are lessened if plan participants have control over their own investments, are provided a wide range of investment options, have sufficient information to make informed investment decisions, and can reasonably reallocate their plan assets.

Of the defined contribution plans, the most popular plans are 401(k) salary reduction plans for larger companies, Keoghs for the self-employed, and simplified employee pension plans for smaller companies, partnerships, and sole proprietorships. Less-used plans include money-purchase plans, stock purchase plans, and thrift plans. Our text will briefly discuss the three most prevalent, SEPs, 401(k)s, and Keoghs. Information on other defined contribution plans is abundantly available.

Again, an investor or financial advisor need not understand every nuance of retirement plans, but it is important to understand their contributions to a total financial plan.

401(k) Salary Reduction Plans

This type of defined contribution plan can be adopted by "C" corporations, "S" corporations, partnerships, and sole proprietorships. Employers and employees contribute to 401(k) plans with pre-tax dollars, thus reducing their current taxes. A plan's assets accumulate tax-deferred until distributed at retirement.

For 1994, employees may defer pretax income of up to $9,240. This maximum contribution amount is indexed each year. Employers may also contribute to an employee's plan account, but combined contributions cannot exceed $30,000.

Plan participants have two choices with regard to employer contributions: receive them in cash or defer the income into their 401(k) account. Nondeferral creates an immediate tax liability. Participation reduces taxes.

Why invest in retirement plans? An example illustrates a major advantage, tax deferral. Matthew Baker and Matthew Wells are rising young attorneys, each with an annual income of $65,000 before 401(k) contributions at the law firm of Baker and Wells. Each is single. Baker takes his employer contributions in cash. Wells defers his employer contribution (see Table 6–1).

Keogh Plans

A Keogh plan is a qualified retirement plan for self-employed individuals. The contributions are deductions and the earnings are tax-deferred until distributed. As with other defined contribution plans, assets can be invested in a variety of investments, since the returns are not guaranteed.

Keoghs are similar to SEPs in most ways except they are more difficult to administer. Keogh plan participant(s) can contribute up to 20% of their compensation up to $30,000.

Table 6–1. Effect of 401 (k) Contribution on Taxable Income

	Baker	Wells
Gross Income	$65,240	$65,240
Less 401(k) Contribution	0	9,240
Taxable Income	65,240	56,000
Standard Deduction (1994)	3,850	3,850
One Exemption	2,450	2,450
Taxable Income	58,940	49,700
Federal Taxes Due (estimate)	11,498	8,911

Investment Note: By combining a profit-sharing plan with a Keogh, a participant can reach the 20% contribution goal.

Simplified Employee Pension (SEP) Plan

The Internal Revenue Code permits a retirement plan making use of employees' IRAs. The SEP provides employees with a simpler alternative to complex retirement plans. Under an SEP plan, an employer contributes directly to the employee's IRA account. SEPs are designed for smaller companies and self-employed individuals. The employer may, at his or her discretion, make annual contributions directly to employee IRAs. The contributions are deductible. SEP contributions do not preclude employees from making IRA contributions.

1994 contributions to SEPs have been reduced to a maximum limit of $150,000 on the income or earnings considered. The new maximum deductible contribution is 15% of compensation or $22,500, whichever is less. For the self-employed, maximum contribution is 13.043% or $22,500, whichever is less.

SEP plans are not required to file IRS reports, furnish the Department of Labor with summary plan descriptions, or furnish employees annual summary reports. SEPs can be established anytime up to the due date of the employer's tax return (including extensions).

Other types of defined contribution plans include:

1. Money Purchase Plan: the employer sets aside a specific amount for the participants annually.
2. Stock Bonus Plan: the employer's contribution is used to buy company stock for the participants.
3. Profit-Sharing Plan: the employer's contribution is usually a percentage of the profits.

Defined Benefit Plans

By definition a defined benefit plan is any plan that is not a defined contribution plan. Defined benefit plans promise participants specific benefits at retirement. In these types of plans the benefits are pre-determined. The variable is the contribution necessary to fund the benefits for the participants.

For example, a participant receives 5% of his or her average annual compensation multiplied by the number of years of service with a maximum of 80% of the annual average compensation:

$$Average\ Annual\ Salary = \$60,000$$
$$Years\ of\ Service = 15$$
$$\$60,000 \times 5\% = \$3,000 \times 15 = \$45,000\ Annual$$
$$Retirement\ Payment$$

Maximum Payment would be $48,000 (80% of $60,000)

Contributions are funded by the employer and the amount of the contributions is determined by an actuary. The actuary must make two primary assumptions: the rate of return of the investments and the rate of growth of the plan participants' compensation. Other considerations could include mortality, participants' ages, interest rates, and employee turnover.

If the plan's assets earn in excess of the projected return and/or compensation increases are below projections, funding requirements are reduced. Conversely, underperforming assets and/or the unanticipated escalation of compensation requirements increase funding requirements.

By whatever name, these types of plans are required to offer benefits that are primarily for lifetime retirement, with specifically determinable benefits, and funding must not depend on the profitability of the employer.

Individual Retirement Accounts (IRAs)

When IRAs were established, every person under age 70 1/2 who received income from employment or self-employment could contribute up to $2,000 (originally $1,500) toward an IRA and the contribution was tax-deductible.

Today, contribution limits are more restrictive and, unlike a 401(k) salary reduction plan, the allowable contribution is a deduction from a participant's adjusted gross income (AGI) on the federal tax return.

While many of today's employees are not eligible for IRA contribution deductions, any employed or self-employed individual can still make a nondeductible contribution to an IRA. However, since the mid-1980s, deductible contributions are subject to the following restrictions:

1. IRA contributions can be deducted only if neither an individual nor his or her spouse is an active participant in an employer-sponsored retirement plan.
2. Their adjusted gross income (AGI) falls below $40,000 filing jointly. A $25,000 limit applies to single persons. Portions can be deducted at somewhat higher levels.

The maximum annual contribution per person is $2,000 or 100% of earnings, whichever is less. A working couple may each contribute up to $2,000, or 100% of their earnings, whichever is less. A $250 contribution can be made for a nonworking spouse, regardless of income.

Retirement Plan Distributions

When a plan participant decides to retire, he or she can receive distributions in one of three ways: a lump sum, regular annuity payments, or transferring the participant's plan assets directly to another plan or IRA. Whatever the participant's decision, it should never be made without seeking the advice and counsel of a retirement planning tax professional or other qualified retirement plan financial advisor. The wrong decision could have serious financial consequences.

Regardless of what distribution option is chosen, taxes will be due on the money received. Monthly distributions will be subject to ordinary income tax as received. Taxes on lump-sum distributions are due immediately. Taxes on IRA rollovers are delayed until the assets are distributed.

One of the least uncomplicated and most beneficial methods of maintaining the value of a retirement plan distribution is to have the assets directly transferred to another plan or IRA. This rollover will maintain the retirement and tax-deferred wealth accumulation benefits of the former plan and delay current tax liabilities. Earnings on the transferred assets also continue to accumulate tax-deferred.

There are a number of considerations regarding the rollover of plan assets to an IRA. If the participant is changing jobs rather than retiring, he or she will want to continue to delay paying taxes, earn tax-deferred, choose the investment vehicles and, if less than 59 1/2, avoid a 10% premature distribution penalty. Equally important, IRA assets can accumulate tax-deferred until the IRA owner reaches 70 1/2. At that point distributions must begin or substantial penalties will apply. The recipient of a lump-sum distribution receives the entire value of his or her retirement account in one payment. The distribution gives the recipient immediate access to all the assets, complete control over all asset investment decisions, and the responsibility for making those decisions.

A lump-sum distribution (not a rollover) also brings immediate tax liabilities. The recipient may gain some relief and address liquidity concerns by electing 5- or 10-year forward averaging. However, future earnings on the balance will be subject to taxation at ordinary income rates as the assets no longer grow tax-deferred.

There are no ironclad rules regarding lump-sum distributions. If the recipient has an income or other financial need, a lump-sum distribution may be appropriate. If no need exists, a recipient is most often better served by keeping the assets in a qualified plan and accumulating wealth tax-deferred. Again, premature withdrawals may be subject to penalties and taxes.

The selection of guaranteed periodic payments is in the tradition of an annuity. The payments may be guaranteed for life and the thesis is that one cannot outlive the guaranteed income. Joint and last survivor benefits are often an option. As an investment advisor, my usual recommendation is not to annuitize unless there are highly unusual circumstances. The major disadvantage is that the annuitization is usually irrevocable and the annuitant loses control over the assets. The money cannot be inherited and the distributions are most often based on conservative earnings projections. Even with these concerns, the biggest disadvantage remains the loss of purchasing power as the guaranteed payments remain the same but the cost of living continues to grow.

Investment Note: A viable alternative to annuitization for special needs is hiring a professional money manager. While not guaranteed, the long-term investment results should be substantially competitive and the money can be passed to one's heirs.

Withdrawal Regulations Common to Most Retirement Plans

1. Retirement plan distributions are generally taxed as ordinary income rates.
2. Withdrawals made prior to age 59 1/2 are subject to an additional IRS tax of 10%.
3. Exceptions to the 59 1/2 age requirement for withdrawal:
   a. The owner is totally and permanently disabled.
   b. Through a trustee "substantially equal periodic payments" are made over the owner's life expectancy.
   c. The IRA owner is deceased and the beneficiary receives the proceeds.
4. Withdrawals must start by age 70 1/2 or the IRA owner will be subject to a substantial excise tax.

Investors must recognize that qualified retirement plans offer outstanding opportunities to build wealth. For investment advisors it is equally important to understand why qualified plans should usually be the first client investment considered. Qualified plans, combined with variable annuities, produce an even more synergistic approach.

As a business owner, one of the biggest breaks available is the ability to invest substantial amounts of deductible money in retirement plans such as SEPs, 401(k)s, and Keoghs.

Nonqualified Plans

A nonqualified plan is an employee benefit that is not eligible for tax advantages, including contribution deductions and tax-deferred wealth accumulation for the recipients. A nonqualified plan can be established without the approval of the Internal Revenue Service (IRS) and is not subject to either nondiscrimination or other qualified plan compliance standards.

This type of plan is established to reward key employees and other highly skilled workers as an incentive to remain with the organization and/or perform work at certain levels. Its significance is the difference between qualified and nonqualified plans and the appropriateness of each, depending on the circumstances.

Summary

- There are qualified retirement plan choices for every size and type of operation, from sole proprietorships to Fortune 500 corporations.
- There are two primary types of qualified plans: defined benefit plans and defined contribution plans. Defined benefit plans guarantee a specific benefit to plan participants, and this is similar to the fixed annuity approach. Benefits from a

defined contribution plan depend on the total contributions and the performance of the plan's investments, and this is similar to a variable annuity approach.

- All qualified plans have similarities, including placing the assets with a trustee, having a written document, having the plan established by an employer, and providing benefits for the plan participants.
- Tax reduction and tax deferral remain the two most important features of qualified retirement plans.
- Plan distribution choices include lump-sum, guaranteed income (annuitization), and rollovers. Unless a participant has a specific financial need, it is most often better to roll over plan assets to an IRA to continue the tax deferral and tax-deferred wealth accumulation.
- Early withdrawal of plan assets before age 59 1/2 can result in substantial penalties and tax obligations. Withdrawals must begin at age 70 1/2 or substantial penalties will result.

How to Purchase a Variable Annuity

As a financial advisor to high-net-worth individuals and corporations for more years than I care to remember, two of my objectives have never changed: to sell only the highest quality products and services and to select the appropriate investments to meet each client's financial and emotional needs. In the financial services industry that is known as needs selling and meeting suitability requirements. To an investor it is known as an advisor doing his job.

In my other life as an investment lecturer, writer, and sales trainer, my message to investment sales representatives and investment advisors is also the same—sell quality products and meet client needs. However, in my presentations I also challenge representatives by asking the questions, Why should an investor select you as a financial advisor? and Why should he or she invest in your recommendation?

An investor will be well served to consider the same approach when making the decision to purchase a variable annuity or any other investment or service. Investors should buy quality products and services, invest to meet their needs, and select an investment advisor who has earned their respect and trust.

Chapter 5 outlines the framework for selecting a financial advisor. The most important criterion is trust combined with the advisor's knowledge, experience, reputation, and institutional affiliation. However, selecting an investment advisor must go beyond mere comfort.

Remember, the variable annuity compensation remains the same, whether it is purchased from an experienced or inexperienced advisor. Hence, a major consideration must be the advisor's working knowledge of asset allocation and risk management. Two other considerations are the representative's approach to customer service and to monitoring post-purchase performance.

However, since many knowledgeable investors make their own investment decisions, why "employ" a financial advisor for the purchase of a variable annuity in the first place?

The reasons are straightforward. First, unless an investor purchases one of the limited number of "no-load" annuities available, a sales commission will be paid regardless of who makes the investment decision.

Second, even many sophisticated investors lack the knowledge required to make an informed decision regarding the purchase of a variable annuity. Variable annuities are complex investment vehicles, and investors may lack the skills necessary to make the initial and continuing asset allocation decisions and to monitor the results once the allocation decisions are made.

Investment Note: Individuals who have sophisticated money management and asset allocation skills (and readers comfortable with the contents of this book) might consider purchasing a "no-load" variable annuity. The advantages and disadvantages of "no-load" variable annuities are briefly discussed at the end of this chapter.

However, as most investors purchase variable annuities from an advisor, our assumption is that an advisor is part of the investor's team. Two other assumptions are made: that the representative will be compensated and that the investor will be subject to a contingent deferred sales charge (CDSC).

Variable annuities are securities sold by licensed, registered representatives. Sales commissions are paid regardless of who makes the investment decision (except "no-loads"). Since representatives will be compensated anyway, it is reasonable to ask their advice and use their often invaluable expertise and services.

An advisor is compensated for giving advice as are other professionals, including attorneys and CPAs. Besides, variable annuity commissions paid to representatives are not paid directly by the investor.

A review is in order to make an investor comfortable with this approach. Commissions are paid to the representative by the insurance company. One hundred percent of an investor's money goes to work immediately. Sub-account purchases are made at net asset value (NAV). The investor is subject to a deferred sales commission only for early withdrawal, not for the initial purchase.

An investment advisor helps you choose a variable annuity to meet your specific investment goals and objectives.

The overriding factor in the variable annuity selection process is determining the safety and stability of the sponsoring insurance company and its ability to meet its contract obligations. The efficient method of screening an insurance company is first to determine its financial rating.

As we learned in Chapter 2, insurance companies are rated on their financial strength and stability by rating services including,

Standard & Poor's, A. M. Best, and Moody's Investor Services. The information is also available in the insurance company's annuity sales literature. There is little reason for an investor to purchase an annuity from any insurance company rated less than investment-grade quality. This is particularly true when purchasing a fixed annuity. The safety of a fixed annuity is guaranteed by the full faith and credit of the company's general account. While general account assets are invested according to strict regulatory guidelines, the fixed annuity assets are not segregated or placed with a trustee.

However, variable annuities offer "double safety": the safety guaranteed by the company's full faith and credit and that secured by placing the sub-account's assets with a trustee. Even in the highly unlikely event of a major insurance company not meeting its contractual obligations, the variable annuity assets are still held in trust, secure and available to the investors.

Once investors understand that safety and security are paramount issues, the need to screen and identify annuities that meet certain quality criteria becomes more apparent. Investors should determine their ratings requirements, outline them to their financial advisors and, in addition, start their own research and screening process.

Advisors have the responsibility to offer competitive products and services. Investment firms and their advisors screen numerous products to select the most appropriate for their clientele. This due-diligence process provides reasonable assurance that the variable annuity contracts selected are competitive and stable.

However, an investor should realize that most investment advisors offer a limited selection of variable annuity contracts. This is not necessarily a negative. As a practical matter, it is impossible for an advisor to offer unlimited investment choices. And be aware that some advisors offer only their own firm's contract. The contract may be competitive, stable, and suitable, but it is prudent for an investor to review several contracts before making a final selection. It is also appropriate to receive proposals from at least two advisors.

An investor's search for the most suitable variable annuity investment opportunity will require determination and a degree of investment sophistication, but it is much easier than one might think. Compare buying a variable annuity to purchasing a car. In an automobile you want certain features, including air conditioning, airbags, automatic transmission, and a CD player.

The same is true when purchasing a variable annuity. Among the important features to evaluate are sub-account choices, money managers, surrender charges, fees and expenses, death benefits, and distribution features. The investor should always compare these types of features and benefits before making a final decision.

Before purchasing a car a potential buyer will visit several dealerships and compare not only features and benefits but also the suitability of the vehicle, its performance record, its cost of operation, and the service available from the dealer. The same process applies to purchasing an annuity. Investors should talk with several variable annuity "dealers" and pick the best "model" before making a final decision.

Financial institutions conduct due-diligence procedures to select investment products and services and for good reason. Satisfied clients purchase additional products and services and refer business associates and friends to the institution. Therefore, it is beneficial for individual investors to understand how financial institutions select investment products, including variable annuities, for their registered representatives to sell. This understanding will assist individual investors in developing their own due-diligence process.

Prior to the sale to clients, a financial institution's due-diligence (research) process determines the viability of products and/or services, their suitability as it relates to the institution's investment policy, and the acceptability of the risk policy of the group(s) managing the investment.

The product selection process begins with the institution—in our case a bank, brokerage, or insurance firm selling variable annuities to retail clients—designing an investment policy that is specific to its needs. For an individual investor it is called determining goals and objectives. The preeminent objective is to select a harmonious group of quality products and services that offer the highest probability of achieving their stated investment objectives. For an individual investor it is called diversification.

The investment policy is also the risk management policy of the institution. Like institutions, most investors are conservative and risk adverse. They are more comfortable when an investment's rate of return is predictable. When given a choice, investors will invariably choose a less rewarding but more predictable investment opportunity. Therefore, most institutions blend their natural tendency toward seeking the maximum investment return within an acceptable level of risk with their customers' need for safety and consistency. For an individual investor it is called determining an acceptable level of risk.

To design an investment policy it is important to understand risk. From a professional money manager's perspective, risk is "the variability of the rate of return" of an individual investment or a group of investments. The cardinal rule of institutional money management is to maximize the rate of return for the level of risk accepted. So should it be for individual investors.

The major limitation of measuring risk is that it is always based on past performance and is measured retrospectively. As all representatives and investors know, "past investment performance does not guarantee future performance." However, investment advisory firms and professional money managers producing consistent and competitive variable annuity sub-account returns offer investors a disciplined and proven method for reaching their long-term investment goals. For an individual investor it is known as selecting a money manager.

Investors are fortunate in that their investment selection process has been narrowed to focus on variable annuities that are selected by their investment advisors. This selection process is further enhanced in that the variable annuities selected by the advisor have also been analyzed and recommended by the institution's due-diligence selection committee. This is a logical and expedient method given the large number of variable annuity contracts that are available.

This double review process, however efficient and credible, must always be followed by an investor's own personal research and evaluation. This includes a perusal of variable annuities not offered by your investment advisor in addition to evaluating those that are.

The most efficient variable annuity evaluation process for either an institution or an individual is a "top down" approach to research. An investor has available extensive research materials from highly professional, insightful sources. These sources furnish the information necessary to make an informed evaluation of most variable annuities. A research source example would be *Morningstar Variable Annuity Performance Report*. Many other sources are also available from public libraries, directly from the advisory services, or from financial advisors and other institutions.

An investor using the "top down" research approach must make two distinct evaluations. First, analyze the insurance company sponsoring the contract. Determine its quality, stability, and reputation. Second, review the sub-accounts' performance results and diversification options. As sub-accounts dictate performance, they should be evaluated as a group to assure sufficient options for consistent performance, asset allocation, and diversification.

Once the quality, flexibility, and general performance issues are resolved to the investor's satisfaction, the contract features and benefits should be examined and compared individually to determine the most suitable variable annuity for the particular needs of the investor.

Each annuity will have some unique and highly competitive features and benefits, but none will have all the "bells and whistles" or be rated truly outstanding when compared with all the other choices. The insurance and money management industries are much too competitive for that to happen. Hence, the decision should be made to purchase the annuity that best meets your specific needs.

Investment Note: Some features may be more hype than substance, and thus of little value to an investor. The question is, are such attractions truly beneficial and do they meet your investment objectives?

While some contracts may have certain unique features, the following features are common to all variable annuities in one form or another:

1. Choice of a specified number of sub-accounts.
2. Money management and money managers.
3. Contingent deferred sales charge.
4. Minimum/maximum purchase requirements.
5. Annual asset management fees.
6. Annual contract charge.
7. Free withdrawal features.
8. Payout options.
9. Free-look period.
10. Number and frequency of sub-account exchanges.
11. Types of purchases allowed.

Evaluating Variable Annuity Sub-Accounts

The three primary securities asset classes for investors are stocks, bonds, and cash. Stock sub-accounts include aggressive growth, growth, balanced, total return, and numerous other combinations of equity investing vehicles that seek capital appreciation as their primary objective. Fixed-income sub-accounts seek income as their primary objective and preservation of capital as a major secondary objective. The investments are primarily government agency, government, corporate, foreign government, and foreign corporate bonds. Bond quality ranges from no-credit-risk U.S. governments to speculative high-yield bonds. Recall that municipal bonds are not included in variable annuities, as their income is already federal and often state tax-free. The third asset class, cash, is defined as money market sub-accounts used as safe havens during turbulent markets or as a temporary "parking place" for funds before reallocation to either stocks or bonds.

When evaluating sub-accounts, three questions arise: How many sub-accounts are available? How many are really necessary? and Are sufficient sub-account investment alternatives available to meet diversification and allocation requirements? Some variable annuities offer 35 to 40 sub-accounts, others offer 5 or fewer, and most fall somewhere in between. An infinite number of choices is desirable but not necessary. A limited number of sub-accounts is more manageable, but will probably not provide the flexibility required to meet long-term investment objectives. The answer as to how many sub-accounts are sufficient, as one might suspect, lies somewhere between too many and too few.

In evaluating sub-accounts it is desirable to pay particular attention to the opportunities for equity (stock) investing. The axiom: Variable annuities are long-term investments; equities will outperform other types of investments over the long term; therefore, a long-term investment portfolio should be weighted toward equity investing.

The fixed-income sub-accounts should include a sufficient number of choices to meet both the investment quality and the competitive yield requirements of an investor's initial and future asset-allocation models. The consummate fixed-income sub-account mix would include: government, government agencies, investment grade corporate, high-yield, foreign government, and foreign corporate bonds. Certain other fixed-income choices would be an additional bonus.

Our third asset class, cash and cash equivalents, is of little consequence to long-term performance except for quality and safety. Variable annuity cash investments should always be short-term for specific reasons including market volatility and reallocation. The major requirement is that a cash sub-account "bucket" be available for temporary investing.

Often, other categories of investments are available. These are specialty sub-accounts that focus on narrow investment niches like individual foreign country equities, natural resources, gold, sectors, and real estate. In the opinion of this writer, these types of investments are not appropriate for most variable annuity purchasers because of their volatility, and thus should not be considered in an evaluation.

Typical variable annuity sub-accounts, objectives, and risks are shown in Table 7–1. Each contract will offer a different grouping of sub-accounts but all variable annuity contracts will include stocks, bonds, and cash. Our example offers 12 sub-accounts. Six are equity, five are fixed-income, and one is a money market. This group of sub-accounts would generally allow an investor to design a diversi-

Table 7–1. Typical Variable Annuity Contract Sub-Accounts Structure

Type of Sub-Account	Primary Objective	Risk Factor
Aggressive Growth	Capital Appreciation	Highest
Global/Foreign Equity	Capital Appreciation	High
Growth	Capital Appreciation	High
Gold	Capital Appreciation	Highest
Natural Resources	Capital Appreciation	High
Balanced	Appreciation/Income	Medium
Government	Income/Preservation	Low
Government Agencies	Income/Preservation	Low
Corporate Inv. Grade	Income/Preservation	Medium
High-Yield	High Income	Highest
Foreign Bonds	Income/Preservation	Medium
Money Market	Income/Safety	Low

fied portfolio to address both specific long-term financial goals and risk tolerance.

Tables 7–2 and 7–3 provide more aggressive and more moderate portfolios designed from our 13 sub-accounts. Again, the number of sub-accounts available must satisfy the investor's asset allocation and risk tolerance level. There is no absolute requirement except a "sufficient" number. Also, sub-account choices are but the first "screen" in

Table 7–2. Examples of More Aggressive and More Moderate Portfolios

	More Aggressive	More Moderate
Stocks		
Aggressive Growth	10%	5%
Global Equity	10%	0%
Growth	35%	25%
Bonds		
Government	15%	25%
Corporate Investment-Grade	15%	20%
Global Income	0%	10%
High-Yield	10%	5%
Cash		
Money Market	5%	10%
Total	100%	100%

Table 7–3. Asset Class Allocation

	More Aggressive	More Moderate
Stocks	55%	30%
Bonds	40%	60%
Cash	5%	10%

our selection process. Equally important is who will manage the money, our next area of discussion.

Money Management and Money Managers

Access to professional money managers is another major benefit of purchasing an annuity. Because money managers offer two major elements that make asset management successful—consistency and long-term results (time)—they offer investors reasonable certainty that they can achieve long-term financial objectives. Consistent returns meet both investment and emotional needs.

Time is important because of the future value of money (compounding) and the present value of money (discounting).

Another key ingredient to successful professional money management is understanding the relationship between risk and reward. All investment decisions present varying degrees of uncertainty, but consequential (that is, high-degree) risk is generally not acceptable to investors. The ability to determine the present value of a future sum allows investors to determine with reasonable certainty how much capital is necessary to invest, as a lump sum or a series of investments, in order to reach specific financial goals.

Meeting long-term investment objectives also requires the proper use of asset allocation (asset class diversification) and, within those asset classes, determining the asset mix of stocks, bonds, and cash to meet the needs of the investor. The allocation of assets is made after considering, among other things, the sub-account investment objective, allowable and acceptable risk parameters, and measurable time horizons. Investors who purchase quality investments that consistently earn above-average returns or even average returns will best serve their own long-term interests.

Therefore, an investor should seek professional managers who have an understanding and working knowledge of, and a clearly defined approach to, producing consistent and competitive performance, asset allocation, risk management, and time horizons.

How does an investor evaluate and select money managers? Fortunately most of the work has already been done. Research firms such as Morningstar, Value Line, and Lipper have available all the information necessary to make an informed decision. Each service is readily available, competitively priced, and recommended by this writer.

An investor's primary mission is to evaluate the investment performance of the variable annuity's sub-accounts over extended periods (e.g., one, three, and five years). The second "screen" is to evaluate the sub-account's performance with sub-accounts having the same investment objective (e.g., equity versus equity). Finally, an investor should use rating service(s) to evaluate the sub-account(s) as an adjunct to other sub-account research.

Succinctly, it is most efficient to use rating and evaluation services for researching the performance of money managers. An investor's responsibility is evaluating and selecting money managers and sub-accounts, not individual securities.

There are three types of sub-account professional money management arrangements:

1. Internal management of all assets.
2. External management of all assets.
3. Combined internal and external management of all assets.

Investment Note: External management may be provided by one investment advisor for all sub-accounts or each sub-account may be managed by an individual investment advisor (the multi-manager approach).

Contingent Deferred Sales Charge (CDSC)

Investors most often are not subject to initial sales charges or front-end sales loads when purchasing an annuity. One hundred percent of the contributions are invested in the sub-accounts at net asset value (NAV). However, investors can be subject to early withdrawal penalties and federal tax penalties as well.

An evaluation of a variable annuity contract should include a clear understanding of the consequences and costs of either early withdrawals or 1035 tax-free exchanges. All contracts basically state that a penalty will be assessed if the assets are withdrawn prior to a certain "maturity" date. Penalties are based on a percentage of assets and the penalty decreases to zero over time as shown in Table 7–4.

Important Information About Contingent Deferred Sales Charges

1. Penalties are generally based on the contributions. However, some penalties are based on accumulated assets. Choose a contract that specifies contributions. It can make a significant difference.
2. Federal tax penalties of 10% are assessed if withdrawals are made prior to age 59 1/2 regardless of the CDSC. Exceptions are death and total and permanent disability.

Table 7–4. Variable Annuity Early Withdrawal Penalties

Number of Years Invested	1	2	3	4	5	6	7	8
Percentage Penalty	7%	6%	5%	4%	3%	2%	1%	0

---

3. Transferring assets from one annuity to another annuity (1035 exchanges), if done institution to institution, will not create immediate federal tax consequences. However, the assets could still be subject to early withdrawal penalties.

Minimum and Maximum Purchase Requirements

Limits are set for both minimum and maximum contributions for the purchase of variable annuities. Limitations vary based on three primary factors:

1. Contribution method: single premium or periodic;
2. Type of annuity: qualified or nonqualified contribution; and
3. Type of contribution: direct contribution or rollover.

Minimum purchase requirements for single-premium, nonqualified, deferred annuity contract purchases are usually higher than other purchase requirements. Minimum requirements are usually even higher for both nonqualified and IRA rollovers (1035 exchanges) and pension plans such as 401(k) plans, profit-sharing, and company pension plans. Initial and subsequent minimum contribution requirements for the purchase of annuities under a systematic purchase plan are less restrictive than single-premium purchases.

Maximum allowable purchases are restricted by the issuing insurance company's underwriting regulations. This does not preclude the purchase of a contract with higher limits, but exceeding the limit does require prior underwriting approval. For example, say an investor wishes to purchase a $1,000,000 variable annuity. Without prior underwriting approval, the company's issuance limit is $500,000. The investor requests and the company approves the higher limit. The $1,000,000 contract is issued.

Investment Note: There are also upper age limit issuance restrictions imposed by insurance companies on the issuance of annuities.

Asset Management Fees

Asset management fees are paid to investment advisors for managing sub-account assets. Because of the large amounts of assets under management, insurance companies are able to offer "economies of scale" or competitive fee schedules to their customers. The management fees charged depend on the complexity of the asset management demands. Foreign equity management requires substantially more research, specialized implementation, and transaction costs than the management of a U.S. government bond fund. Asset management fees reflect those differences. Equity sub-account fees are higher than bond sub-account fees.

Fee comparisons are particularly important. Every dollar charged comes directly from the performance profitability of the sub-account. Remember to compare the proverbial apples to apples: in this case, similar equities to equities sub-accounts and similar bonds to bonds sub-accounts (see Table 7–5).

Table 7–5. Fee Comparisons: Various Sub-Accounts

Sub-Account	Annual Performance	Management Fees	Net Performance
Foreign Equities	14.35%	1.25%	13.10%
Emerging Growth	12.50%	1.00%	11.50%
Growth	10.00%	0.70%	9.30%
Investment-Grade Bonds	7.80%	0.65%	7.15%
High-Yield Bonds	9.25%	0.75%	8.50%
Foreign Bonds	9.25%	0.90%	8.35%

Annual Insurance Company Expenses

Annuity contracts include charges for insurance companies' annual expenses. In addition to the asset management fees, there are three other annual charges: annual policy fee, mortality and expense risk, and administrative.

Annual Policy Fee (Maintenance Fee)

An annual fee, usually $50.00 or less, is charged for the maintenance of the annuity records. The fee pays accounting, customer reporting, and other general expenses associated with financial record-keeping requirements.

Mortality and Expense Risk

An annual charge, 1.00 to 1.50% of the daily asset value of each sub-account, is charged for the mortality risk that arises from the obligation to pay guaranteed death benefits or guaranteed lifetime income payments to annuitants.

Administrative Fee

An annual fee, usually 0.15% or less of the daily sub-account asset value, is charged to reimburse administrative expenses.

Variable Annuity Accumulation and Distribution Phases

There are two phases of the "life" of an annuity. The initial phase is the accumulation phase. This is the period in which contributions are made, either as a lump-sum or in systematic payments. The contributions are invested in either a fixed or variable annuity. The assets compound tax-deferred until the contract owner makes the decision to distribute (distribution phase) the assets, either in a lump sum or systematically.

There are two primary methods for purchasing an annuity: a lump-sum purchase and a systematic purchase. With a lump-sum purchase, an investor purchases a variable annuity with one payment. This type of purchase is generally made by more affluent investors seeking tax-deferred wealth accumulation. As previously discussed, lump-sum purchases are usually subject to minimum initial purchase requirements.

Many investors build wealth through systematic purchases of sub-account investment units. This method is called dollar-cost averaging and is the cornerstone of many investment programs. The method dictates that the investor purchase fixed dollar amounts of variable annuity sub-accounts (units) at regular intervals, without regard to price. When prices are high, fewer units are purchased. Conversely, when prices are low, more units are purchased. The net result is that the average cost of all shares bought is lower than the average of all prices at which purchases are made. A program stressing dollar-cost averaging is a long-term investment strategy. It does not guarantee that the investor will make profits. Risks, however, are reduced by the systematic approach to investing.

Through the annuity process, in return for the variable annuity purchase, the insurance company guarantees that the annuitant will receive either a series of payments or a lump-sum payment, or a combination, at a later date. Until the distribution date, the funds are invested in sub-accounts and grow tax-deferred. The total payments to the annuitant(s) will depend on the amount contributed, the rate of return on the funds, how long the money has been invested, the distribution guarantees, and the number of annuitants.

Free Withdrawal Features

Most annuities offer systematic and periodic withdrawal (monthly, quarterly, annually) options to annuity investors. These withdrawals are not subject to surrender penalties unless they exceed a certain percentage of the annuity value during a certain period, usually a contract year.

Annuity distribution options vary widely. Many contracts have common features. An investor should determine his or her own retirement or estate funding needs and decide accordingly. (Chapter 2 outlines some common features of most contracts.) The most important considerations are reasonable liquidity and allowable withdrawal frequency. This is particularly important to investors seeking a monthly income for retirement. Also remember that a 10% penalty may be assessed on withdrawals if the annuitant is under 59 1/2 (IRS penalty).

Selected Annuity Settlement Options

Numerous settlement options are available to the annuitant during the distribution phase. Options range from receiving a lifetime income to having a beneficiary receive the entire proceeds after the death of the annuity owner. There is no "best" distribution choice. The option chosen will depend on the annuitant's financial needs and investment philosophy. Traditionally, annuities have been purchased to provide a lifetime retirement income. Now, however, more sophisticated and innovative annuity contracts have given investors additional incentives for purchasing annuities, including retirement, wealth accumulation, and estate planning.

Settlement options compare favorably to the risk-reward scenario of the stock and bond markets. As fixed returns and guarantees increase, periodic distribution amounts decrease. For example, an annuity that pays the annuitant for life with no minimum number of payments guaranteed (life certain) will distribute larger periodic payments than an annuity guaranteeing a minimum number of payments even if the annuitant dies (life annuity with period certain).

The four most common settlement options are described below.

Life Annuity (Lifetime Income)

The annuitant is guaranteed a lifetime income. At the death of the annuitant all payments cease and the annuity is without value. No minimum number of payments is guaranteed.

Advantage: Payments are maximized for the life of the annuitant.

Disadvantage: At the annuitant's death the annuity has no value to his or her beneficiary (estate).

Life Annuity with Period Certain

The annuitant receives a lifetime income but a minimum number of payments are made whether the annuitant lives or dies. The annuitant receives two guarantees: a certain amount will be paid periodically for the lifetime of the annuitant; and, should the annuitant die prior to the time-certain guarantee being satisfied (usually 5 to 20 years), the annuitant's beneficiary will receive the remaining number of guaranteed payments.

Advantages: The annuitant will receive a lifetime income. A minimum number of periodic payments will be made.

Disadvantages: The longer the guaranteed payments, the less the periodic payment. Beneficiary payments stop after the guaranteed time payment.

Joint-and-Last-Survivor Annuity

Periodic payments are guaranteed for the lifetimes of two or more annuitants. Payments continue until the death of the last annuitant. The joint-and-last-survivor option is typically used by a husband and wife seeking a guaranteed joint lifetime income and then a guaranteed life income for the surviving spouse.

Periodic payments are made for the life of one person until his or her death. At that point, the survivor becomes the annuitant and payments are made until the death of the survivor. The periodic payments are usually less (3/4 to 1/2 the initial amount) to the surviving annuitant.

Advantage: The annuitants are guaranteed a lifetime income.

Disadvantages: The periodic payment amount is less for two or more annuitants. The periodic payment is usually reduced for the surviving annuitant(s).

Lump-Sum Payment

The annuitant has the option of receiving the entire value of an annuity in a lump sum or in self-determined periodic amounts. This allows the annuitant to maintain control of the corpus, the distribution(s), and the tax liabilities.

Advantage: The annuitant retains complete control of the annuity value.

Disadvantages: The annuitant is not guaranteed a lifetime income. Withdrawals may deplete the corpus. Possible tax and penalty consequences.

Contract Designations

A primary benefit for the variable annuity investor is the right to decide its ownership, beneficiary, and distribution method. The designations of owner, beneficiary, and annuitant are made at the time of purchase. They can be changed at the owner's option. These are important decisions and should be considered carefully.

There are many contract designation combinations and options available to investors. Table 7–6 applies to nonqualified annuity contracts; the two illustrations are the most common choices. The examples assume that the owner(s) die before the date of annuitization (income date).

Table 7–6. Two Examples of Contract Designations

Example 1

Intent:	Ownership by Husband (Wife)
	Husband to Receive Annuity Payments
	Wife Receives Ownership at Husband's Death
	Children Receive Contract After Both Parents' Death
Owner Designation:	Husband
Annuitant:	Husband
Contingent Annuitant:	Wife
Beneficiary:	Wife
Contingent Beneficiary:	Children

When the husband dies, the wife becomes the new owner and annuitant. She may surrender or continue the contract. At the mother's death, the children can keep the contract for up to five years.

Example 2

Intent:	Husband and Wife Are Joint Owners
	Husband to Receive Annuity Payments
	One Spouse Becomes Owner at Death of Other Spouse
	Children Are Beneficiaries
Ownership Designation:	Joint
Annuitant:	Husband
Contingent Annuitant:	Wife
Beneficiary:	Children

Free-Look Period

Each state requires that the annuity investor be given a specific period of time to examine and evaluate the contract after it is issued and delivered. The minimum period for most states is 10 days, though some have longer examination periods. Should the purchaser decide to cancel, in most states he or she will receive the greater of the purchase price or the value of the accumulation account, less certain charges for mortality and expense risk, administration fees, and state taxes. As this requirement is dictated by state statute, it provides one more opportunity to examine a contract and determine that the features and benefits promised are included therein.

Sub-Account Reallocation

Allocating assets to various sub-accounts is appropriate and essential when determining the best risk-reward "mix" to reach long-term investment objectives. Most annuity contracts allow more than a sufficient number of reallocations during a given period, usually one year. The investor should make sure that allocations are available at any given time, not just quarterly or annually.

The Variable Annuity Death Benefit

Insurance companies frequently stress the value of the guaranteed death benefit offered by their variable annuity contracts. Contracts guarantee that, upon the death of the annuity owner, the beneficiary receives either the value of the contract or 100% of the contributions, whichever is greater. An additional benefit of many contracts is a step-up feature in which the contract death benefit is increased after a certain number of years to reflect the most current value of the contract.

While this is comforting, an investor should realize that the overall benefit can be modest. For example, an investor purchases a $100,000 annuity. Market losses decrease its value by $5,000. The owner dies. The investor's beneficiary receives $100,000, of which $5,000 is an insurance benefit and $95,000 is a return of investment.

As with most long-term investments, a more likely scenario is that the investor will live for a number of years, the variable annuity will increase in value, and the investor's beneficiary will receive the contract's value. However, it is a reassuring feature that a beneficiary will never receive less than the investor's total contributions.

The Variable Annuity Evaluation Checklist

1. Rating of the Variable Annuity Insurance Company
   Rated Investment Quality or Better

2. Number and Types of Sub-Accounts Available
   Minimum Number of Sub-Accounts Required
   Number of Equity Sub-Accounts
   Number of Fixed-Income Sub-Accounts
   Money Market Account

3. Long-Term Performance of Sub-Account Types
   Aggressive
   Growth
   Balanced
   Government Bond
   Investment-Grade Bond
   High-Yield Bond
   Money Market

4. Deferred Sales Charges
   Number of Years Before No Contingent Deferred Sales
   Charge (CDSC)

Percentage Early Withdrawal Penalty Charged Each Year
Penalty Based on Total Contributions or Total Assets

5. Minimum Contributions Required to Purchase
Initial Minimum Lump-Sum Contribution Required
Initial Minimum Periodic Contribution Required
Continuing Minimum Contribution Required

6. Asset Management Fees and Other Expenses
Sub-Account Investment Advisor Fees
Mortality and Expense Risk
Annual Policy Fee
Administrative Fee

Other features and benefits vary in their importance, but the two most critical considerations for selecting a variable annuity are sub-account performance and contract expenses. The evaluation process allows investors to compare variable annuities in these two critical areas. By using industry research sources such as Morningstar, Inc., plus their own independent research, investors can determine if a contract's sub-accounts are producing consistent and competitive performance. An investor can also determine if the expenses charged for asset management, mortality and risk, and administration are competitive or excessive.

Purchasing a No-Load Annuity

Purchasing a no-load variable annuity is similar to purchasing no-load and "B" share mutual funds. Most variable annuity contracts charge no "front-end" load or sales commission. One hundred percent of an investor's contribution is invested at NAV in the sub-accounts. However, in most instances, expenses and charges are higher for variable annuities distributed by institutions where the sales representative is compensated by commission, just like mutual funds. This being the case, why not purchase a no-load variable annuity?

An investor with the ability to manage money, allocate assets, make independent investment decisions, and monitor sub-accounts might consider purchasing a no-load variable annuity. However, before an investor makes that decision, he or she should consider the following:

1. Financial advisors are an invaluable resource in selecting and monitoring variable annuities.
2. Financial advisors add more value than the additional fees.
3. The number of no-load variable annuities available is presently very limited.
4. Annual insurance company expenses are lower.
5. No-load annuities are sold without early withdrawal penalties.

No-load variable annuity availability will continue to grow. It is the writer's opinion that no-loads certainly have a place in the variable annuity arena. The only question is the contribution of the investor's financial advisor. Most often his or her guidance and expertise is worth the nominal additional expense. As always, however, the final decision rests with the investor.

Summary

- Investing in a variable annuity is the same as purchasing any other product or service. The investor should evaluate need, reputation, quality, and service.
- Selecting an investment advisor is an important part of the variable annuity process. Since a sales commission will be paid to the advisor selected, it is important to investigate the advisor's industry credentials, experience, reputation, and institutional affiliation.

- Purchasing an annuity from an insurance company that is rated as a "quality" or investment-grade company is important. The company's financial stability assures security.
- Fixed annuities are guaranteed by the full faith and credit of the company. Variable annuities are guaranteed by the company's full faith and credit in addition to the sub-account assets being placed with a trustee. This is known as "double safety."
- Buying a variable annuity is similar to purchasing a car. There are many different models with many different features. The investor should decide on his needs and seek a variable annuity that meets those needs and offers the appropriate features and benefits.
- The total number of sub-accounts becomes less important than their diversification. It is important to have sufficient equity and fixed-income sub-accounts to meet asset allocation needs. Additional sub-accounts can contribute but are not critical.
- The requirement of the contingent deferred sales charge (CDSC) is an important consideration when purchasing an annuity. Even though variable annuities are long-term investments, circumstances could require an early withdrawal. The shorter the time period and the smaller the penalty percentage, the more beneficial the CDSC.
- Annual fees and expenses make a difference in performance. All costs are charged directly to the sub-accounts. Smaller expenses mean better overall performance.
- Free withdrawal features are important even if the investor does not intend to withdraw the assets. Again, circumstances change and it is always nice to have the option. The same can be said of payout options. The more options the better.
- Remember, unless there are unusual circumstances, annuitization of a variable annuity is not appropriate.

- Investors get a 10-day "free look" to make absolutely sure the annuity contains all the promised features and benefits that were promised. An investor is well served to evaluate the policy again during this period.
- Most variable annuity contracts allow more than a sufficient number of sub-account exchanges. Check your options before purchase and remember that you are a long-term investor, not a market timer.
- When deciding whether to purchase a no-load or an annuity sold by a sales representative, this writer recommends using a financial advisor for the many reasons contained in this chapter.

8

TAX-ADVANTAGED INVESTING

KEY CONCEPTS

▼ The Advantages of Qualified Retirement Plans

▼ The Advantages of Municipal Bonds

▼ The Three-Tier Tax-Advantaged Approach to Investing

▼ Strategic Tax-Advantaged Planning

A number of financial objectives take priority over tax-deferred annuity growth. These include making the maximum contributions to retirement plans, eliminating credit-card and consumer debt with high interest rates, establishing and maintaining a cash emergency fund, endowing educational needs, and considering the benefits of tax-free income. However, once these goals are achieved, an investor should give serious consideration to including a variable or fixed annuity in a well-designed, well-diversified, long-term investment strategy. Also, retirees should give earnest thought to using variable or fixed annuities for tax-deferred growth, financial security, and estate planning.

As we have seen, variable annuities provide investors with an effective method for meeting long-term investment objectives through tax deferral, professional money management, and asset allocation. Tax deferral allows the accumulation of assets without creating current tax liabilities. Professional money management provides consistent, competitive returns. Asset allocation reduces investment risk through asset class diversification. The variable annuity is most beneficial when it is part of an investment strategy that includes qualified retirement plans, tax-advantaged investments, and growth-oriented investments. This diversification, combined with an adequate time horizon, will provide an investor with a competitive return, an acceptable level of risk, and favorable long-term investment results.

Again, it is important that investors understand that, ideally, the purchase of a variable annuity is part of a comprehensive investment strategy, not a panacea for wealth accumulation and/or retirement funding. Remember:

1. Retirement planning and wealth accumulation are complementary processes, not isolated investment strategies.
2. Asset allocation combined with a sufficient time horizon will produce successful investment results.
3. Risk is dissipated by asset diversification and time.

Tax-Advantaged Asset Allocation Investing

Since you will probably employ a financial advisor, you might as well make her earn her commissions and/or fees by discussing all the tax-advantaged opportunities available to investors.

The first item on the agenda is to determine what investments are germane to your long-term financial objectives and which are not. From our "top-down" research approach we have learned that all investors should consider consistency, quality, vendor reputation, advisor expertise, risk, and investment suitability. We have also learned that an investor must clearly understand the relationship between risk and reward. The risk will vary according to the type of investment. The opportunity for gain should be in direct proportion to the risk assumed.

Within that research framework an investor must also consider asset allocation. This is not a foreign concept—each month most investors allocate short-term (cash) assets to categories that include mortgage, insurance, automobile, education, and utility payments. For other investors the allocation involves country club dues, travel, investments, and gifts to grandchildren. In each instance the principle is the same. The primary difference is the affluence and the priorities of the person allocating the assets. Investment allocation among securities works in the same manner except the choices are limited to stocks, bonds, and cash.

For the purposes of building a well-diversified portfolio of tax-advantaged investments—one that offers capital gains, tax-free income, and tax-deferred income—we will consider three primary opportunities: qualified retirement plans, municipal bonds, and annuities. We will also discuss the tax advantages of individual equities and certain types of mutual funds.

Qualified Retirement Plans

Many currently employed investors make contributions to tax-advantaged qualified retirement plans. It is not an option for retirees. However, since many retirees have assets in qualified plans, this chapter also includes a retirement plan withdrawal strategy for retirees.

Table 8–1. Net Cost of $2,000 IRA (30% Tax Bracket)

Investor Contribution	$2,000
30% Tax Savings	(600)
Net Cost to Investor	1,400

The first investment employees should consider is a qualified retirement plan. The contributions are tax deductible, the assets grow tax-deferred until distributed, and employers often contribute additional funds. When IRAs were available to any working individual regardless of income, the logic that convinced clients that it was an outstanding opportunity was straightforward. Consider an investor in the 30% tax bracket. If he will invest $1,400, the U.S. government will add $600 and the $2,000 will grow for him without being taxed until he retires. Few investors turned down the opportunity. (See Table 8–1.)

IRA investment benefits are now more limited. However, qualified retirement plans offer an even more beneficial opportunity to build assets for retirement. As discussed in detail in Chapter 6, retirement plans offer immediate tax benefits and tax-deferred compounding, as detailed in Table 8–2.

Unless it is financially unfeasible, there is very little reason why an employee should not build wealth through qualified retirement plan contributions. Table 8–2 demonstrates the growth of a single contribution. The results of annual contributions for the 20-year period are even more dramatic. Employer contributions also contribute to this wealth accumulation.

Table 8–2. The Immediate Tax Benefits and Tax-Deferred Compounding of Retirement Plans

Step One—The Immediate Benefit

Investor Taxable Income	$100,000
Retirement Plan Contributions	(10,000)
Investor Net Taxable Income	90,000
Assuming 28% Marginal Tax Rate	
($9,000 × 28%) Tax Savings	2,800

Step Two—The Long-Term Benefit

Invest *$10,000 Tax Deferred Compounded* at 10% for 20 Years
Versus
Invest *$10,000 at 28% Taxable Compounded* at 10% for 20 Years

$10,000 Investment

	Tax Deferred		28% Taxable	
Year	10% Interest	Principal plus Interest	10% Interest Less 28% Tax	Principal plus Interest
1	$1,000.00	$11,000.00	$ 720.00	$10,720.00
2	1,100.00	12,100.00	771.84	11,491.84
3	1,210.00	13,310.00	827.41	12,319.25
4	1,331.00	14,641.00	886.99	13,206.24
5	1,464.10	16,105.10	950.85	14,157.09
6	1,610.51	17,715.61	1,019.31	15,176.40
7	1,771.56	19,487.17	1,092.70	16,269.10
8	1,948.72	21,435.89	1,171.38	17,440.48
9	2,143.59	23,579.48	1,255.71	18,696.19
10	2,357.95	25,937.43	1,346.12	20,042.31
11	2,593.74	28,531.17	1,443.05	21,485.36
12	2,853.11	31,384.38	1,546.95	23,032.31
13	3,138.43	34,522.71	1,658.32	24,690.63
14	3,452.27	37,974.98	1,777.73	26,468.36
15	3,797.50	41,772.48	1,905.72	28,374.08
16	4,177.25	45,949.73	2,042.93	30,417.01
17	4,594.97	50,544.70	2,190.02	32,607.03
18	5,054.47	55,599.17	2,347.71	34,954.74
19	5,559.92	61,159.09	2,516.74	37,471.48
20	6,115.91	67,275.00	2,697.95	40,169.43

Distribution Strategy for Retirees

Qualified retirement plan distributions have certain rules and restrictions that must be considered when withdrawing funds from the retirement plan to maximize the benefits to the investor.

There is a minimum and a maximum age limit for distributions. Withdrawals before age 59 1/2 are subject to a 10% IRS penalty in addition to the ordinary income due on the distribution. Exceptions include disability and certain other specified reasons. Withdrawals must begin, either in a lump sum or in periodic payments, and contributions must cease, at 70 1/2.

Withdrawal options may include:

1. Lump-sum distribution (all at once)
2. Regular payments determined by your life expectancy
3. Periodic sums larger than based on your life expectancy

Regardless of the method chosen, the annual distribution amount must at least equal assets divided by life expectancy. As an example, assume an IRA with $120,000 in assets owned by a male 70 1/2 years old.

$$\frac{\$120,000}{12\text{-Year Life Expectancy}} = \$10,000 \text{ Minimum Annual Withdrawal Required}$$

Failure to withdraw sufficient funds will result in a 50% excise tax on the underdistributed amount. Distributions are taxed at ordinary rates. (See Table 8–3.)

Most retired investors considering the purchase of a variable annuity have well-funded retirement strategies that include one or more of the following: Social Security benefits, company pension, interest income, tax-free income, and dividends from equities. All the current income is taxed at ordinary income rates except the

---

Table 8–3. IRA Distribution: Insufficient Funds Withdrawn

Distribution Required	$12,000
Actual Distribution	10,000
Underdistributed Amount	2,000

$2,000 × 50% = $1,000 Excise Tax Due

---

municipal bond tax-free income, and that is counted in Social Security calculations.

Unless the income is needed to fund retirement expenses, it is usually advantageous to roll-over the plan assets to an IRA at retirement and let the assets continue to grow tax-deferred until the time when the assets are needed or at age 70 1/2 when distributions are mandatory. Remember, you can withdraw the assets any time. Distributions are subject to ordinary income taxes at the time of withdrawal.

Investment Notes: There is no advantage to rolling over retirement plan assets to a variable or fixed annuity. The assets are already growing tax-deferred. Purchasing an annuity would unnecessarily make the assets subject to early withdrawal penalties and additional fees.

The author recognizes that purchasing a single-life or joint-and-last-survivor annuity is a distribution option, but it is never recommended unless unusual circumstances and specific needs prevail.

Municipal Bonds

Municipal bonds (or munis) are debt obligations issued by various state and local municipal entities. The most attractive feature of municipal bonds is that all the interest (income) from the bonds is federally tax-free. In certain instances it is also state tax-free.

The bonds are issued as general obligations (GO) of the issuer or are issued for special projects of an issuer, such as a water/sewer system, and the debt is retired from the revenue of the project. A general obligation bond is backed by the full faith, credit, and taxing power of the issuer. Bonds are rated by municipal bond rating services including Moody's and Standard & Poor's. The ratings range from AAA to C. Most individual investors purchase investment-grade bonds (BAA or better), but more speculative bonds (rated BBB or less) are also available.

There are a number of variations of individual municipal bonds and municipal bond funds. Both vary according to quality, maturity, location (various states), and objectives, but the underlying factor is that every fund seeks income that is federally tax-exempt.

A typical investment objective of a tax-free municipal bond fund would be monthly income exempt from federal income taxes, from a select portfolio of investment grade municipal bonds. The other general types of municipal bond mutual funds are:

1. *Long-term municipal bond funds* invest in bonds issued by states and municipalities to finance schools, highways, hospitals, airports, bridges, water and sewer works, and other public projects. The fund generally purchases municipal bonds with longer maturities because they often offer higher yields. (Municipal bond funds can also be short-term maturities.)

2. *State municipal bond funds* work like any other municipal bond fund except their portfolios contain the issues of only one state. A resident of that state has the advantage of receiving income free of both federal and state taxes. Funds are offered with both long-term and short-term maturities. These funds can be particularly beneficial to residents of states with high personal income taxes, such as California.

3. *Tax-exempt money market funds* invest in municipal securities with relatively short maturities. These are also known as short-term municipal bond funds.

An individual can invest for tax-free income by purchasing either individual municipal bonds, municipal bond funds, or municipal bond unit trusts. Investors with substantial resources and investment expertise often purchase individual municipal bonds. Most tax-free investors purchase municipal bond mutual funds. A limited number of investors purchase unit trusts.

Sophisticated buyers who purchase individual municipal bonds receive higher returns versus mutual funds (no management fees), determine their own bond-rating requirements, decide what maturities are most suitable, and select the locality of the issuer. In exchange they assume the asset management responsibility and usually reduce their overall diversification.

Municipal unit investment trusts (MUITs) purchase a fixed portfolio of tax-free municipal bonds. Individual units in the trust are sold for approximately $1,000. Unit holders receive an undivided interest in both the principal and the income portion of the portfolio in proportion to their investment. The portfolio of securities remains fixed until all the municipal securities mature and the unit holders' principal is returned.

Unless an investor has a substantial municipal bond portfolio, she is usually better served by purchasing mutual funds because they offer professional money management and diversification. Unit trusts are not favored by the author because of their fee structure and lack of active management.

Regardless of how investors purchase municipal bonds, they purchase them for one reason: tax-free income. They are compatible with retirement plans and annuities and can combine to make an outstanding tax-advantaged total investment strategy. The basis for purchasing municipal bonds is evaluating and comparing the net yield to the investor. The equivalent taxable yield concept is demonstrated in Table 8–4.

It is important to know how and why an investor purchases municipal bonds. In the case given in Table 8–4, a 3% real return is

Table 8–4. Municipal Bond Tax-Free Investing

How to determine the taxable equivalent of a municipal bond.

$$\text{Yield Equivalence} = \frac{\text{Dividend}}{(100 - \text{tax bracket*})}$$

* On state funds include the state tax rate to calculate the equivalent yield.

A $10,000 municipal bond and a $10,000 corporate bond of equal quality and similar maturity pay the following rates.

	Annual Return
Corporate Bond	8.00%
Municipal Bond	6.50%

The question to be answered is, Which bond is a better purchase for a California investor in the 39.6% federal tax bracket? The answer is the bond that offers the best "net" return to the investor.

	Corporate Bond	**Municipal Bond**
Annual Return	$800	$650
Taxes at 39.6%	(317)	(0)
Net Return	483	650
Assume 6% California Income Tax*	(48)	(0)
Net-Net Return	435	650

* State of California Bond

The answer to the first question is that the municipal bond is the better investment. The second question is, What is its real rate of return?

Net Return Versus Rate of Inflation (CPI)

Net Municipal Bond Return	6.5%
Inflation Rate (CPI)	(3.5%)
Positive Rate of Return	3.0%

a good and acceptable reason. Furthermore, the municipal bond is a better buy than the corporate bond paying a higher yield. The best news of all is you now know the reasons, but aren't worried—you have professional money managers to make those decisions.

The Tax Advantages of Equity Investing

Purchasing growth stocks is an excellent method for wealth accumulation and tax deferral. While the value of a stock investment might grow substantially, no taxes are due on the gains until the stock is sold. For affluent investors the long-term capital gains are favorable compared to the ordinary income tax rate.

However, most investors will be more comfortable with our three-tier, tax-advantaged approach to investing. "Picking" individual stocks for long-term growth is a major talent indeed. It requires extensive research, sufficient capital, patience, and a calm demeanor.

Most individuals investing in equities should consider our solution for everything from a bad cold to becoming wealthy and beautiful: hire professional money managers and invest in growth mutual funds. You may pay some capital gains taxes along the way but it is the safe and sensible approach to tax-advantaged equity investing. Besides, it "mostly" works.

The Tax-Advantaged Approach to Investing

Level One: Qualified Retirement Plans

Advantages:

> Contributions are pre-tax dollars
> Earnings grow tax-deferred
> Additional contributions by employer

Disadvantages:
>   Early withdrawals subject to penalties
>   Often have limited investment options
>   Limited contributions

Level Two: Tax-Free Municipal Bonds (Bond Funds)
Advantages:
>   Interest is federally tax-free
Disadvantages:
>   Purchasing power risk (inflation)
>   Market risk (value depreciation)
>   Contributions not deductible

Level Three: Private Pensions (Variable Annuities)
Advantages:
>   Earnings accumulate tax-deferred
>   Guaranteed death benefit
>   Retirement planning flexibility
>   Unlimited contributions
Disadvantages:
>   Funded with after-tax dollars
>   Early withdrawals subject to penalties

>   See Figure 8–1 and Table 8–5.

Summary

- Variable annuities should be an integral part of a total financial plan, including the elimination of short-term consumer debt, retirement plan contributions, and cash emergency funds.
- Retirement planning and wealth accumulation are complementary processes. Each should include asset allocation and

Figure 8–1. Tax-Advantaged Approach to Investing

Variable
Annuities

Nonqualified Tax-
Advantaged Investments

Retirement Plans – Core Investments

Adequate Time Horizon   **Diversification**

a sufficient time horizon to produce successful investment results.

- Tax-advantaged asset allocation investing is not a new concept. Individuals allocate short-term assets (cash) each month by paying their monthly bills. The concept is expanded to three-tiered, tax-advantaged investing that includes retirement plans, municipal bonds, and variable annuities.

- A qualified retirement plan is the first investment an individual should consider. The contributions are tax-deductible and the contributions accumulate tax-deferred.

- Retirees maintaining assets in qualified retirement plans have several distribution strategies that can maximize the benefits of their plans.

- Municipal bonds are classified as general obligation (GO) and revenue bonds. Their quality and maturity dates vary. One feature common to all municipal bonds is federally tax-free income. Many are also state tax-free. The measured value

of a municipal bond is its yield as it relates to a positive net rate of return.
- Individuals can invest in municipal bonds one of three ways: through individual bonds, mutual funds, or unit investment trusts. Mutual funds are the suitable vehicles for most investors.
- Purchasing equities for long-term capital appreciation is another opportunity to accumulate wealth tax-deferred.

Table 8–5. Comparison of Variable Annuities, Mutual Funds, and Municipal Bond Funds

	Variable Annuities	Mutual Funds	Municipal Bond Funds
Tax-Deferred Accumulation	Yes	No	Yes
Rate Guaranteed	No	No	No
Reinvestment of Earnings	Yes	Yes	Yes
Market Risk	Yes	Yes	Yes
Early Withdrawal Penalty	Yes	No	No
Principal Guaranteed	No	No	No
Possible IRS Penalties	Yes	No	No
Surrender Penalties	Yes	Possible	No
Short-Term Investment	No	Possible	No
Liquidity	Yes	Yes	Yes
Long-Term Investment	Yes	Yes	Yes
Inflation Hedge	Yes	Yes	Possible
Periodic Investing	Yes	Yes	Yes
Settlement Options	Yes	No	No
Lifetime Income	Yes	Possible	Possible
Death Benefits	Yes	No	No
Probate	No	Yes	Yes

Investment Note: Interest from municipal bonds is federally tax-free, not tax-deferred. Principal is returned when individual municipal bonds mature.

Unless an investor is an experienced stock "picker," he or she should hire mutual fund money managers to invest their equity assets.

- Three-tiered, tax-advantaged investing includes qualified retirement plans, municipal bonds, and variable annuities in an asset allocation model constructed to accumulate wealth and reduce risk.

9

Asset Allocation and Risk and Reward: A Practical Application

Key Concepts

▼ Asset Allocation

▼ Diversification

▼ Risk and Return

▼ Standard Deviation as a Decision-Making Tool

The adage, "If you're so smart, how come you're not rich?" has more truth than one might imagine. Most smart investors do become rich or at least very comfortable financially. By the same token some very highly educated, dynamic, articulate, and otherwise brilliant people do some really less than brilliant things when it comes to managing their assets. As an investment advisor, I find it amazing how often high-profile, high-income individuals seek my advice on how to reorganize their disastrous financial affairs. Equally amazing is the number of more-modest-earning individuals seeking my advice who own their home, have no appreciable debt, and have retirement plans, savings accounts, and other investments valued in the hundreds of thousands of dollars.

There are no major secrets to becoming a smart investor and accumulating wealth. The winning combination for becoming rich (slowly) is invest early, invest often, purchase good quality, live within your means, maintain an emergency fund, have some patience, and don't do really stupid things with your assets. Those modest-earning individuals slowly accumulating wealth understand sacrifice, discipline, common sense, and consistency. That is the road to wealth accumulation. Some of our equally hardworking professionals understand one-half of the concept: earn money. The breakdown comes with the translation of the second half of the concept: systematically save and invest money.

In order to become financially independent it is important to have investment "savvy," or in our case, (Wall) street smarts. In previous chapters we discussed the ten investment basics and three-tiered, tax-advantaged investing.

Now it is time to take the capstone course and blend our "techie" knowledge with some logical, commonsense investing methods. Some additional study is required: asset allocation and its relationship to risk. However, this chapter also deals with sensible investing, avoiding investment mistakes, and how a commonsense approach blends with variable annuity investing.

We practice asset allocation in our everyday lives. Each month individuals allocate a portion of their current assets to mortgage and utility payments. The reward is maintaining a residence. The risk for nonpayment is loss of services or foreclosure. Mortgage and utility payments are essential. Everyone understands the essentials risk and reward scenario; the rewards are obvious and the consequences are clearly defined.

Consumer discretionary spending is also clearly understood when the decisions affect our daily lives. Do we spend our entertainment money on dinner at Billy Bob's House of Ribs or do we order in pizza, rent a video, and save a few bucks? Straightforward and measurable rewards, with identifiable costs and little risk. Investment contributions are also discretionary allocations. The primary difference is that investing and saving are a reallocation of assets, not an expense. You keep the assets as part of your net worth.

It is important to understand the difference between required and discretionary spending and short-term and long-term investing.

Unlike short-term individual essential and discretionary spending, our focus is on the discretionary assets available for investing to meet long-term objectives that include retirement planning and wealth accumulation. Once these resources are identified, our goal is to allocate them in the most efficient manner possible within our acceptable risk levels.

Asset Allocation

Asset allocation as it relates to variable annuities should not be confused with diversification. Asset allocation is our allocation of assets to three primary areas: stocks, bonds, and cash. By distributing our assets in these three basic areas, the probability that a portion of our assets will be in the "right place at the right time" is reasonably assured.

Further, a higher, long-term, total investment return will be realized because of the lack of asset concentration in one investment classification. This produces more consistent returns. Finally, risk is reduced because asset allocation spreads the risk over all categories.

For our purposes, diversification relates to the choosing of subaccounts in our variable annuity contract. The decisions are made after the stocks, bonds, and cash percentages are determined. Consider the following asset allocation example:

1. 60% allocation of sub-account assets to equities
2. 30% allocation of sub-account assets to bonds
3. 10% allocation of sub-account assets to cash

Diversification of equities example:

1. 20% allocation to aggressive growth sub-account
2. 20% allocation to global equities sub-account
3. 60% allocation to blue-chip sub-account

The significance is that 100% of the equity investment is 60% of the total portfolio. The equity positions are diversified within their asset class and the classes are diversified by asset allocation.

Investment Note: Our selections are limited to sub-accounts, as the selection of individual securities remains with the sub-account managers.

Why is asset allocation important to investors? Because the proper allocation of investment assets within a securities portfolio is considered by most professional money managers as the principal ingredient for successful investment performance. This, combined with specific investment selections, risk management, and interpretation of economic and other market influences, forms the basis for successful money management and satisfied investors.

As we have illustrated, asset allocation is simply apportioning investment assets among various categories. The asset allocation determination is made without regard to specific securities. The true test of asset allocation is determining the overall mix that, when combined with proper security selection within each asset category, meets the investor's needs within his or her acceptable risk-tolerance level.

Most investors are conservative, risk averse, and most comfortable with a consistent rate of return. Asset allocation generates more consistent returns and more predictable risk forecasts.

However, asset allocation is not all-encompassing. As with all financial strategies, the investor must consider income, time horizon, capital appreciation, risk concerns, and the interrelationships of each consequence within a total investment strategy. For example, a 100% fixed-income portfolio is suitable for a short-term investment horizon. However, a nondiversified fixed-income portfolio for long-term investment horizons is often not appropriate. It usually satisfies the investor's safety "comfort" level, not the investment objective of maximizing returns within an acceptable risk-tolerance level.

Again, investors must understand that asset allocation and diversification reduce, rather than increase, risk. Investors can serve themselves well by becoming educated on the dynamics of inflation and the need for risk reduction.

Portfolios can be designed to address many variables. Using asset allocation to meet investor objectives need not be complicated. It can be as straightforward as designing basic portfolios using simple asset allocation alternatives, as demonstrated in Figures 9–1 and 9–2 and Table 9–1.

Risk Reduction through Diversification

As Table 9–2 shows, depending on the investor's risk tolerance, an investor could use an asset-allocation model to reallocate the assets of a 100% fixed-income or 100% equity portfolio. It illustrates that diversification increases total return or reduces risk, or both. The table shows that an investor who diversifies into a 50/50 stocks/bonds portfolio mix receives a higher return for the same amount of risk.

Risk and Return

The concept of risk and reward is the cornerstone of the investing process. Investment decisions should not be made without considering both. All investments involve an element of risk and an anticipated or expected return. Risk should be measured and quantified to determine its compatibility with predetermined investment objectives.

Figure 9–1. Asset Allocation Model—Growth Portfolio

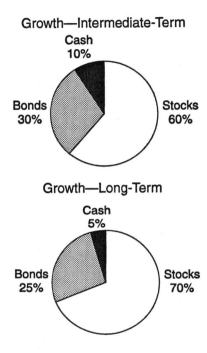

Growth—Intermediate-Term

Cash 10%

Bonds 30%

Stocks 60%

Growth—Long-Term

Cash 5%

Bonds 25%

Stocks 70%

Table 9–1. An Asset Allocation Portfolio Matrix

	Conservative	Moderate	Aggressive
Bonds	80%	60%	25%
Stocks	15%	35%	70%
Cash	5%	5%	5%

Figure 9–2. Asset Allocation Model—Balanced Income Portfolio

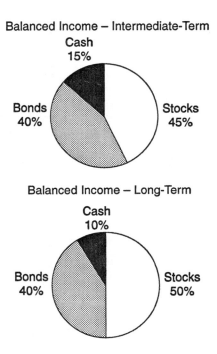

Balanced Income – Intermediate-Term

Cash 15%

Bonds 40%

Stocks 45%

Balanced Income – Long-Term

Cash 10%

Bonds 40%

Stocks 50%

What is risk? Risk, in investment, is the exposure to the chance of loss. To investors, risk is the probability of a loss in either the market value (the price decreases) or the income stream (dividends) or both. There are at least four basic risks that an investor should consider: business, market, interest-rate, and price risk. Of the four, three are important to understand when investing in sub-accounts.

Table 9–2. Asset Allocation Models

	Annual Return	Risk Measurement
Stocks (100% invested)	10.0%*	12.0%*
Bonds (100% invested)	7.0%*	9.0%*
Stocks/Bonds Mix (50%/50%)	9.0%*	9.0%*

*For illustration purposes only. Risk/reward and returns depend on the asset classes, sub-accounts, and securities chosen.

Business Risk

Income declines due to a number of reasons indigenous to the business environment. This is important to money managers when making individual securities investments. It is less important to investors who have hired money managers to analyze the risk of individual securities. It is important for investors purchasing individual securities.

Market Risk

The market value of sub-account portfolios may vary substantially over short time periods. Market risk dissipates over time, and variable annuities are long-term investments. However, declines in market prices obviously reduce an investment's value.

Interest-Rate Risk

The value of fixed-income securities and interest rates varies inversely. Interest rate fluctuations can dramatically affect bond values and CD rates. Rising interest rates cause falling bond prices. Fixed-income investment unit values decrease during periods of sharply rising interest rates.

Inflation Risk

This is the most powerful risk an investor faces. Purchasing power risk is the risk that an investment's value will be eroded through inflation. Inflation risk is a major threat to fixed-income investments, particularly CDs.

Measuring Risk

Professional money managers seek the maximum return for a given level of risk. Conversely, they seek the lowest risk for a given level of return. A rational investment strategy dictates that investment options be ranked according to risk. Thus, the risk should be measured and quantified.

Measuring some risk is intuitive. Investors understand that an aggressive technology stock has more risk than a Treasury bill; that the chance of winning a coin flip is infinitely higher than winning the state lottery; that the odds of winning the lottery are remote but the reward is high; and that Treasury bills pay single-digit but secure returns. All investors understand obvious risks and their counterbalance, the reward opportunity.

Unfortunately, the differences of investment risk are not so clearly defined. For instance, which is a better buy given their levels of risk and return: domestic aggressive growth or Pacific Rim equities? Your investment decisions are most often about either asset-allocation (stocks, bonds, cash) models or mutual fund and/or sub-account investing because of your choice of professionally managed investments.

However, an investor should understand that various variable annuity sub-accounts have different risk-reward scenarios. For example, an aggressive growth sub-account has a higher risk-reward potential than a government bond sub-account. That being the case, how does an investor evaluate risk and reward as it relates to sub-account investing?

The investment industry has devised measurements for each. They are known as alpha (reward) and beta (degree of risk). Alpha is your expected return for the level of risk assumed. Beta measures the quantified risks over a given time period. In each case there will be variance, which is measured by the standard deviation. This anticipates the upside and downside potential at a given level of risk.

Alpha is important when measuring and comparing sub-accounts and money manager performance. First, performance should be measured over a specified period of time. Second, it should be measured and compared to its peers and industry averages.

The statistics in Table 9–3 indicate that the Equity XYZ sub-account:

1. Had a positive return for five consecutive years.
2. Outperformed its market index four of five years.
3. Was ranked in the top 20% for equity sub-accounts for five consecutive years.
4. Was in the top 10% of all equity sub-accounts in the third year of comparison.

In summary, for its investment class, equities, it is an excellent choice. Unfortunately, making the buying decision for most sub-accounts is not as clear-cut. This type of decision is made much easier by using investment performance research materials from various sources, including Lipper, Morningstar, and Value Line.

The beta coefficient is one method of measuring risk. It relates the volatility of an investment to the market as a whole. The market, or

Table 9–3. Alpha Measurements: XYZ Sub-Account

	Year				
	1	2	3	4	5
Return	12.2	10.5	3.6	11.6	14.5
Equity Index	11.5	11.5	1.2	10.0	13.8
Rank Among 60 Funds	12.0	20.0	6.0	11.0	15.0

Illustration only: not actual data.

measurement index, has a beta of 1.00. A sub-account with a beta greater than 1 has more risk than the market portfolio because its return is more volatile than the market. A sub-account with a higher beta would usually be classified as a growth or aggressive growth sub-account. Sub-accounts with betas less than 1 are more defensive and are often balanced or investment-grade, fixed-income sub-accounts.

Beta risk is an important consideration for professional money managers and investors alike since the effective use of diversification can reduce residual risk. Beta derivation is a straightforward concept. Most sub-account betas are accessible to investors through numerous industry research publications and ratings services. Table 9–4 shows that, if the Dow Jones 30 Industrial Average increases by 10% for a given period, agressive growth will increase by 14% and equity/income by 8%.

Table 9–4. Equity Beta Coefficient Illustration The Market Index—Dow Jones 30 Industrial Average

Sub-Account	Beta
Aggressive Growth	1.40
Foreign Equities	1.30
Growth	1.20
The DJIA Market Index	<u>1.00</u>
Blue Chip	1.00
Equity/Income	0.80
Blue Chip/Balanced	0.70

Beta 1.00	=	Market Beta
Beta greater than 1.00	=	More risk: growth or aggressive growth
Beta less than 1.00	=	Less risk: investment-grade, fixed-income

---

Lifecycle Beta

Beta can also be a measure of risk for an investor's stage in the life-cycle and general attitude toward risk. There is no quantifiable measurement for either, as both are obviously subjective. However, commonsense dictates that preservation of capital is more important to older investors, while growth is usually more important to younger investors.

Table 9–5 assumes an investor who is a reasonable risk taker. Thus, his personal Beta is 1.20 from age 20–54. However, the age beta automatically adjusts his risk tolerance downward despite his risk attitude. Investors should determine their own risk levels—this illustration is for an aggressive investor.

The Importance of Standard Devation

An in-depth discussion of standard deviation is beyond the scope or purpose of this text. Our purpose is to give variable annuity investors a clear understanding and practical approach to understanding the risk-reward relationship.

Table 9–5. Age Beta—Aggressive Investor Beta Illustration

Age	Age Beta	Risk Attitude	Average Beta
20–29	1.40	1.20	1.30
30–39	1.30	1.20	1.25
40–49	1.20	1.20	1.20
50–54	1.00	1.20	1.10
55–62	0.90	1.00	0.95
62–70	0.40	0.90	0.65
70–Up	0.30	0.70	0.50

Source: Southeast Capital Management. By permission.

By definition, standard deviation is the opportunity for gain versus the possibility of a loss at a given level of risk. As an example, there is a 20% chance that an expected return of 20% will be attained by investing in Florida Life's equity sub-account. There is a 30% chance of a 15% return, 20% chance of a 10% return, 20% chance of a 12% return, and 20% chance of a 10% loss. Should you invest in the sub-account? (See Tables 9–6 and 9–7.)

Table 9–6. Expected Return Illustration

Occurrence	Probability	Return	Calculation
1	.20	20%	4.00%
2	.30	15%	4.50%
3	.20	(10%)	(2.00%)
4	.20	10%	2.00%
5	.10	12%	1.20%
Expected Return		9.70%	

Table 9–7. Standard Deviation

Occurrence	Probability	Return	Deviation	Squared	Probability × Squared
1	.20	20%	10.30%	106.09	21.22
2	.30	15%	5.30%	28.09	8.43
3	.20	(10%)	(19.70%)	388.09	77.62
4	.20	10%	0.30%	0.09	0.02
5	.10	12%	2.30%	5.29	0.53
Variance					107.82
Standard Deviation (Sq. Root of Variance)					10.38

The Practical Application

The practical application of standard deviation is that an investor can make a reasonable assumption that the investment return will approximate 10.70%. However, he may also assume that with 68% (one S/D) or 95% (two S/D) certainty what the best- and worst-case scenarios will be for his investment. (See Table 9–8.)

In making business and personal decisions it is effective to ask, "What is the best event that could happen, what is the worst event that could happen, and what will probably happen?" The same method is an outstanding approach for making investment decisions.

Assume that we are considering allocating assets to the BFW equity/income sub-account and the BFW investment-grade bond sub-account. How do we begin? We don't have sufficient information to calculate performance probabilities, nor is it necessary. We simply review XYZ's performance in a research source and make an allocation determination. (See Table 9–9.)

Intuitively we can determine that in the worst-case scenario neither investment should have a major negative annual return. We expect that their performance will continue to be reasonably consis-

Table 9–8. Best- and Worst-Case Scenarios for Investment Return

	68% Certainty		Expected	95% Certainty	
	Best	**Worst**		**Best**	**Worst**
XYZ	20.08%	(0.68%)	9.70%	30.46%	(11.06%)

Table 9–9. XYZ Performance

	Year					
	1	**2**	**3**	**4**	**5**	**Average**
BFW E/I	10.2	1.3	9.6	11.3	10.3	8.54%
BFW Bonds	6.8	7.1	5.2	9.1	7.2	7.08%

tent and that the sub-accounts will be well managed regarding preservation of capital. Our best-/worst-case total return for E/I ranges from 15% to –5%. For bonds the range is 10% to –3%.

Also, we know that our investment strategy is long-term. In year two, our equity/income sub-account had a 1.3% total return. Overall, however, it has performed well, with a five-year average return of 8.54%. The bond sub-account has also been consistent, with a five-year average return of 7.08%. Are both good investments? Make a final comparison: how did the sub-accounts perform versus their peer group? Consider the following information:

BFW Equity/Income	Current Year Performance Rank	6 of 42
BFW Inv. Bonds	Current Year Performance Rank	20 of 50

The answer is yes, they are competitive. Both perform well when compared to similar sub-accounts.

Investment Strategy

It is important that investment advisors give clients a realistic evaluation of the worst-case scenario. As an example, in the recent difficult bond market, our recommendation to sophisticated investors was an equal exposure to high-grade foreign, U.S. government, and domestic high-yield bonds. Our worst-case scenario prediction was a 5% total return loss. The bad news was that it happened (down 4.5%). The good news was that our investors knew the risks, were disappointed but not surprised, and continued with the long-term program.

Integrating Risk and Return

The concepts of risk and return have been analyzed as separate entities. Synergism is created when they are measured together. Sophisticated investors understand the positive correlation between risk and return. Increased risk should offer increased return. Conversely, returns decrease as risk decreases.

An investor may expect a safe (riskless) return of five percent by purchasing risk-free investments such as short-term Treasury bills. Increasing our expected return above five percent, however, involves the assumption of risk.

The relationship between risk and reward differs between investors and with the ever changing business environment. However, with sophisticated investors, the relationship is always positive.

Summary

- There are no major secrets to successful investing. The winning combination includes an early start, regular investments, quality products, a modest lifestyle, an emergency fund, patience, and common sense.
- Individuals practice asset allocation in their everyday lives by disbursing assets in order of their priorities. Essential expenses (mortgage) are paid first, followed by discretionary spending (entertainment). Investing is a discretionary asset allocation function. The decisions include short- or long-term time horizon, amount for each investment category, and regularity of contributions.
- Asset allocation as it relates to variable annuities disburses assets to three primary areas: stocks, bonds, and cash. This assures that a portion of an investor's assets will be "in the right place at the right time."
- Diversification deals with the allocation of assets among various security classifications. For example, within the equity securities' classification are aggressive growth, growth, and balanced.
- The true test of asset allocation is meeting investor needs for more consistent returns and predictable risk forecasts.

- There is a direct relationship between risk and reward. For every unit of risk taken by an investor, a proportionate unit of reward should be received.
- Risk, the exposure to the chance of loss, is measurable, though not an exact science.
- Alpha measures return. Beta is an excellent method for measuring risk. A beta of 1.00 measures the "market." A beta more than 1.00 is more aggressive than the market. A beta less than 1.00 is less aggressive than the market.
- Standard deviation is a good indicator of worst-case, best-case, and most likely scenarios. A clear understanding of the maximum risks is particularly important to investors.
- Many research sources are available for making performance, asset-allocation, and risk-assumption investment decisions. Their use is highly recommended.
- Risk and reward should be considered and measured together. The appropriate level of risk-reward is an individual decision, but is made easier by proper research and evaluation.

10

THE VARIABLE
ANNUITY PROSPECTUS

The Annuity Prospectus

Despite rumors to the contrary, a variable annuity prospectus is definitely readable, relatively easy to understand, and provides the information necessary to make an informed buying decision. It will also educate potential investors on the nuances and specifics of the variable annuity contract, including the annuity's purpose, investment options, method of payment, charges, fees, and settlement provisions. It provides useful information about the sub-accounts and their investment objectives. Working knowledge of the prospectus helps determine an annuity's suitability for meeting long-term investment objectives, and results in realistic expectations about its features and benefits.

This chapter deals with three aspects of the prospectus: first, the terminology of the contract; second, the equity and fixed-income sub-account investment options and their relative risk and reward; and, finally, a checklist for systematically evaluating variable annuity contracts.

The first step is receiving the prospectus itself. The variable (or fixed) annuity prospectus should be current (effective). By regulation, a current prospectus must be given to investors considering a variable annuity. This legal requirement assures that investors have access to the most current information about the particular variable annuity. The initial step in becoming "prospectus literate" is to understand the terminology of the prospectus.

Important Terms

Annuity prospectuses include a glossary of important terms of the contract. Understanding them enhances an investor's ability to evaluate the features, benefits, choices, fees, and terms of an annuity.

Accumulation unit: A unit of measurement to determine the value of each sub-account unit, determined by the same process as the NAV of mutual fund shares.

Annuity option: The traditional name of the investment. Specifically an annuity is a series of regular payments based on the life of the annuitant. The most common payment options are life, life with a period certain, and/or joint and last survivor. The annuitant makes the decision to annuitize.

Annuitant: The individual on whose life the contract is issued.

Contingent annuitant: The person who becomes the annuitant at the death of the first annuitant under certain circumstances. The designation is part of the contract. It is made prior to the commencement date of the annuity.

Beneficiary: At the death of the contract owner or annuitant, the person(s) who receives the existing value of the contract.

Code: The Internal Revenue Tax Code sections in effect and applicable to the current terms outlined in the prospectus.

The Commission: The Securities and Exchange Commission. The government agency of primary jurisdiction for investments. Note: state security and insurance commissions also regulate the sale of fixed and variable annuities.

Contract value: The combined value of the sub-accounts and/or the fixed account of the contract.

Fixed account: Part of the general account that offers a guaranteed (fixed) return.

Fixed annuity: An annuity that provides a fixed and guaranteed payment for the life of the contract. The payment structure varies according to the option(s) selected.

General account: The account that contains all the assets of the insurance company other than the assets of the variable annuity separate account.

Joint ownership: More than one owner of a contract. Joint owners have equal ownership rights and each must authorize the exercising of any contract rights.

Nonqualified contracts: Contracts issued that do not receive favorable tax treatment under IRS Code Sections 401, 403(b), and 408. Contributions are not tax-deductible, but still grow tax-deferred.

Qualified contracts: Contracts that receive favorable treatment under IRS Code Sections 401, 403(b), and 408. Contributions are deductible and grow tax-deferred.

Sub-account: Account established within the separate account including stocks, bonds and other nonguaranteed return accounts.

Sub-account transfers: Outlines the number and terms of "switches" allowed and the conditions for transferring all or part of the assets of one sub-account to another.

Variable annuity: An annuity that provides regular payments with the distribution amount based on the performance of the underlying separate and sub-accounts.

The Contract

The prospectus outlines the general and specific terms of the contract. Some contract terms vary according to the individual. General conditions of all contracts include the following.

Eligibility: Contracts are generally available to individuals and groups and on a qualified or nonqualified basis. Many insurance companies offer several types of contracts to meet both group and individual needs.

Age: Most contracts restrict the maximum issue age, with ages 75 to 85 being the industry range. An investor age 70 or above should make certain of the maximum issuing age and any restrictions or exclusions that could circumscribe the contract.

Premiums: The minimum, initial premium for a nonqualified fixed or variable annuity ranges between $1,000 and $5,000 depending on the issuer. In group and qualified annuity plans, the minimums are generally less. Contracts provide for either a single payment or a series of payments. Minimum and continuing payment requirements are determined by each individual company. An investor should determine his or her annuity funding method prior to purchase.

Investment options: Fixed annuities have one option for investing: a guaranteed fixed rate. However, some insurance companies offer a series of maturity dates. Under a normal yield curve, the longer the annuity fixed-rate maturity date, the higher the guaranteed return. Variable annuity choices can vary from 5 to 20 or more sub-accounts, depending on the contract. The major choices remain stocks, bonds, and cash (fixed account). The investor should determine the appropriate number of sub-accounts preferred and their asset mix prior to purchase.

Fees: Each contract specifies a fee structure. Included are mortality, money management, administrative, and other nominal charges deemed appropriate.

Contingent sales charges: Generally, annuity contracts do not charge initial sales commissions (loads). However, most contracts have provisions for penalties for early withdrawal.

Maturity date: Every annuity contract has a specified maturity date at which distribution payments begin. Most contracts allow for a deferral period past the maturity date.

Death benefit: In the event of the death of the contract owner prior to annuitization, the insurance company will pay the annuity beneficiary the contract's accumulated value, less withdrawals, or the amount of premiums paid, less withdrawals, whichever is greater. Variable annuity contracts never pay beneficiaries less than 100% of the premiums paid.

Free-look period: All annuity contracts are required by state regulation to offer an investor a "free-look" provision. The purchaser has a period of 10 to 20 days after purchase to return the contract. However, the return of the contract can still result in certain fees, mortality charges, and market losses absorbed by the investor.

Free withdrawals: To address the issue of liquidity, most contracts offer a nonpenalty withdrawal option. Commonly, after the first year, 10% can be withdrawn annually without penalty. Another common option is the nonpenalty withdrawal of the accumulated earnings at any time. Note: withdrawals can be subject to an IRS 10% penalty for withdrawals prior to age 59 1/2. Also, withdrawals subject to taxation are taxed at ordinary income rates.

Annual statement: By statute, all companies must provide an annuity contract owner with an annual statement that provides information on all account activity. It is important for the annuitant to review the annual statement to determine the previous year's "net" return and the current value of the annuity.

General and Fixed Accounts

Variable annuities are divided into two accounts: the general account and the separate account. The general account contains all the assets of the insurance company, including the fixed account. The fixed account may be structured in a manner similar to a fixed annuity with laddered maturities, a guaranteed fixed rate, and a guaranteed return of principal. The full faith and creditworthiness of the insurance company is based on the assets of the general account. The type and manner in which the assets may be invested are highly regulated by state insurance commissions.

Separate Accounts

The separate account is set apart from the general account and is the "umbrella" account for all the sub-accounts of the variable annuity. The separate account is not insured by the issuer of the annuity except in the event of the contract owner's death. It should also be noted that separate account assets are not attachable by creditors should the issuer become insolvent (a highly unlikely event).

Major Sub-Account Investment Objectives

The types of sub-accounts available in variable annuities are as diverse and numerous as the number of contracts available. The primary purpose of the sub-accounts is to offer the contract owner sufficient investment choices to design an asset-allocation model that addresses specific, long-term investment objectives.

Aggressive growth. Seeks above-average capital appreciation by investing in emerging growth and more speculative common stocks (equities). Current income is not an objective.
Comparative beta: 1.40.

International. Seeks above-average capital appreciation through the purchase of foreign securities, primarily common stocks. Current income is not an objective. The sub-accounts are also subject to foreign currency and interest-rate fluctuations. Global funds include foreign and U.S. securities.
Comparative Beta: 1.50.

Small capitalization. Seeks aggressive capital appreciation by investing in small capitalization and emerging growth stocks. Highest category of equity investment risk. Current income is not a consideration.
Comparative beta: 1.60.

Equity growth. Seeks capital appreciation by investing in higher-quality common stocks. Moderate current income is a secondary objective.
Comparative beta: 1.20.

Blue-chip growth. Seeks conservative capital appreciation by investing in quality, blue-chip stocks. Current income is a secondary objective. Consistency and preservation of capital are also "unofficial" objectives.

Comparative beta: 1.00 (the market).

Balanced. Seeks conservative capital appreciation by investing in high-quality, dividend-paying stocks combined with fixed-income securities (bonds). Preservation of capital is a secondary objective. Consistent performance is preferred by the investors of balanced sub-accounts.

Comparative beta: 0.80.

Table 10–1 provides a summary of comparative betas.

Major Fixed Income Sub-Accounts Investment Objectives

U. S. Government Securities. Seeks competitive current income and the preservation of capital through investing in U.S. Government and U. S. agencies' obligations. Governments are subject to market risk, but not credit risk.

Table 10–1. Comparative Equity Sub-Account Betas[*]

Small Capitalization	1.60
International	1.50
Aggressive Growth	1.40
Equity Growth	1.20
Blue-Chip	1.00

[*]For comparative purposes only. Not actual data.

Source: Southeast Capital Management, Inc., Estimates and Evaluations Division.

Investment-grade corporate bonds. Seeks current income consistent with the preservation of capital, with capital appreciation a secondary investment objective. Invests in high-quality corporate bonds.

High-yield bonds. Seeks to maximize current income with capital appreciation a secondary objective by investing in lower-grade corporate bonds. This type of sub-account contains high risk.

Money market. Seeks high current income, preservation of capital, and liquidity by investing in money market instruments.

See Table 10–2 for a risk-reward comparison.

Table 10–2. Fixed-Income Risk-Reward Comparisons[*]

	Market Risk	Credit Risk
U.S. Government		
Short-Term Maturity	Lowest	None
Medium-Term Maturity	Moderate	None
Long-Term Maturity	Higher	None
Inv.-Grade Corporate		
Medium Maturity	Moderate	Moderate
Long Maturity	Higher	Moderate
High-Yield	Highest	Highest
Money Market	Lowest	Low

[*]For comparative purposes only. Not actual data.

Source: Southeast Capital Management, Inc., Estimates and Evaluations Division.

Variable Annuity Prospectus 10-Point Evaluation Checklist

1. Insurance Company Quality Rating

An investor should only purchase an annuity from an insurance company with an investment-grade rating. This is particularly important with a fixed annuity. It is guaranteed only by the insurance company's full faith and credit and its general accounts assets, not assets placed in trust.

Variable annuities have a double layer of protection. First, the variable annuity assets are guaranteed by the full faith and credit of the insurance company. Second, all separate account and sub-account assets are placed with a trustee to guarantee safety.

2. Sub-Accounts Availability

A variable annuity should offer sufficient equity, bond, and money market choices to meet an investor's asset-allocation and risk-tolerance levels. An investor should pay particular attention to the number of equity sub-accounts available, since stocks generally outperform fixed-income securities over a longer time period. Variable annuities are long-term investments.

3. Money Managers

Consistent and competitive performance is critical to the overall success of variable annuity wealth accumulation. There are three primary money management programs available: internal asset management; external money management; and a combination of both. Each approach is acceptable if the sub-account's performance is satisfactory.

4. Sub-Accounts' Past Performance

It is important to evaluate the sub-accounts' performance as a group. As the assets will often be allocated to a number of sub-accounts, overall consistent performance is more important than a few stellar performers.

5. Fees and Expenses

All fees and expenses are subtracted directly from the sub-account assets. Every dollar paid in contract charges reduces performance proportionately. Hence, fees and expenses are an important consideration. The following fees and expenses should be evaluated:

Variable account annual expenses
Mortality and expense risk charge
Administrative expense charge
Contract charge
Sub-account annual expenses
Management fees
Other expenses

6. Contingent Deferred Sales Charges

Variable annuity investors are not subject to front-end loads or initial sales commissions. However, investors can be subject to substantial penalties for early withdrawal of sub-account assets. Depending on the contract, contingent deferred sales charges (CDSC) are eliminated over a 5- to 10-year period. The CDSC structure is a major consideration.

7. Death Benefit

All contracts guarantee payment to the beneficiary of 100% of the contract value or the total amount of contributions, less withdrawals, whichever is greater. Realistically, the death benefit is not a major benefit, particularly after the first few contract years. The logic? After a relatively short time, a variable annuity's contract value will invariably exceed the investor's total contributions. Otherwise why purchase an annuity?

Some contracts offer an additional death benefit feature that an investor might find attractive. After a certain number of years, typically five or more, the guaranteed death benefit is adjusted upward to reflect the contract's increased value. For example, by the fifth year anniversary an initial $100,000 variable annuity contribution has grown in value to $150,000. On the anniversary date the $100,000 guaranteed death benefit is increased to $150,000.

Again, the increased death benefit's value decreases as the annuity continues to grow in value over time. The lesson? Don't choose an annuity based on its insurance protection provision—it is not a major factor.

8. Liquidity (withdrawal features)
Liquidity is very important to investors planning to use annuity assets to fund retirement. It is less important to those seeking only to accumulate tax-deferred wealth and avoid immediate taxation. However, investor circumstances can change. Investors should give preference to contracts that offer reasonable distribution terms.

9. Sub-Account Transfer Regulations
Unlimited transfers between sub-accounts for asset-allocation models may appear to be a major benefit. However, most long-term investors make relatively few sub-account "switches" except during severe market conditions or when investment objectives change. Contracts that allow three or more reallocations annually are usually more than adequate.

10. Settlement and Annuitization Options and Distributions
The appropriate question about settlement options is not, What options are available? but, Does an investor really want to annuitize? The short and loud answer is no—unless there are highly unusual circumstances.

The problems with annuitization are that the decision is irrevocable, the annuitant loses control of the assets, the guaranteed periodic distribution is usually less than the return from personally investing the money, and the annuity contract value for beneficiaries is zero at the annuitant's death.

My opinion is that retaining control of the contract's assets is a better deal for the contract owner. If circumstances require protecting a minor and/or an incapable person, a guardian and/or trustee should be considered versus annuitization. The care is personalized, the assets are invested and available, and the corpus can be passed to heirs.

First-In First-Out (FIFO) Rule

All distributions from an annuity prior to the maturity or annuitization of the contract are treated, until all interest is distributed, as a return of interest (earnings) and are taxed as ordinary income. Once 100% of the interest has been distributed, the remainder is distributed as a nontaxable return of principal. (See Table 10–3.)

Table 10–3. Example of FIFO Rule

Example: An SPDA contract is purchased for $100,000. The value of the contract increases to $150,000 in 10 years. Assume that the contract owner is 59 1/2 or older and that there are no applicable deferred sales charges.

Initial Investment:	$100,000
Appreciation:	$50,000
Total Value:	$150,000

Withdrawals:	
1.	$40,000 (ordinary income)
2.	$10,000 (ordinary income)
3.	$50,000 (principal return)
4.	$50,000 (principal return)

Summary

- The prospectus is an invaluable tool for educating investors on the features, benefits, investment options, fees, expenses, and other specifics of the variable annuity contract.
- To evaluate an annuity contract, an investor should acquire a working knowledge of its important terms and conditions. The contract contains all the pertinent information necessary to make an informed investment decision.
- There are two types of major accounts for annuities: general and separate. The general account contains all the assets of the insurance company except the assets in the separate account. The separate account is the conduit to the variable annuity's sub-accounts. All assets of the separate and sub-accounts are held in trust by a trustee.
- Variable annuity sub-accounts offer a wide array of investment choices in the areas of stocks, bonds, and cash. Each sub-account has a beta or volatility market measure. Risk increases with an increase in a sub-account's beta.
- Only government securities are without credit risk. All fixed-income securities have market risk.
- A variable annuity should be evaluated prior to purchase. There are at least 10 major evaluation checkpoints that should be considered before a final decision is made.
- For reasons already argued, the author considers the annuitization of an annuity contract not in the best interest of the contract owner.
- Nonannuitized annuity distributions are taxed at ordinary income rates until 100% of the interest is distributed. The balance is distributed as a nontaxable return of principal.

11

ANSWERING THE MOST ASKED INVESTOR QUESTIONS

KEY CONCEPTS

▼ Variable Annuity Investor Concerns

▼ Long-Term Tax-Advantaged Planning

▼ Realistic Variable Annuity Expectations

▼ Variable Annuity Financial Planning Benefits

There are three approaches to purchasing a variable annuity: seek the recommendation of a financial advisor; conduct personal research; or a combination of both. In any case, adequate knowledge about variable annuities will make the purchase a less intimidating and more satisfying experience.

An investment advisor's ideal clients understand the features, benefits, and advantages of an investment. They also appreciate the advice and contributions of the professional advisor. Informed investors are able to determine the suitability of a variable annuity and to evaluate the contributions of the advisor.

Most questions asked by investors concerning variable annuitues focus on seven primary areas: stock market risk, performance, fees, liquidity, personal income taxes, the long-term investment commitment, and safety and guarantees. In this chapter, using a question and answer interview format, we will answer those questions and respond to other concerns of annuity investors. This is our less formal, "quick-start" approach to variable annuity and most other types of long-term investing.

Statement: "I don't want to tie my money up for a long time, I'm 65 years old."

Response: Most investors underestimate their life expectancy by a number of years. As an example, at age 65, a male investor's life expectancy is 19 years (female 22 years). Twenty years from now an investor will still need a competitive return and tax advantages. In addition, annuities have numerous distribution options that will address liquidity needs.

Question: "I buy CDs because they are insured. Is a variable annuity and its return insured?"

Answer: No, it is not guaranteed. We are talking about two different classes and types of investments. Annuities are long-term growth investments.

CDs are short-term, fixed-income investments. CDs offer short-term liquidity and safety coupled with long-term exposure to inflation. Variable annuities have some exposure to short-term market risk coupled with a long-term, tax-deferred wealth-accumulation opportunity.

The real risk for an investor is inflation. CDs do not address this issue. Over 5- to 10-year periods, equities have always outperformed fixed-income investments, especially CDs.

Fixed annuity rates and return of principal are guaranteed by the full faith and credit of the insurance company. Like variable annuities, their earnings grow tax-deferred until withdrawn.

Question: "How safe is the variable annuity and the company issuing it?"

Answer: An investor's assets are safe; however, it is always recommended that any insurance company selected be rated investment-grade, for example, A+, one of the highest ratings for safety.

All the variable annuity sub-account securities are held by a trustee or custodian. So, even in the most unlikely event of the financial collapse of a highly rated insurance company, an investor's money is still safe. This is the annuity's "double protection" safety feature.

Statement: "I only invest in mutual funds."

Response: Variable annuities and mutual funds are complementary investments, not mutually exclusive. Mutual funds are also excellent investments for accumulating wealth. Variable annuities complement mutual funds, but with the advantage that all the earnings triple compound tax-deferred.

Investing for long-term growth in retirement plans is also recommended. Like variable annuities, they also offer tax-deferred wealth accumulation.

Statement: "I prefer tax-free to tax-deferred."

Response: Like mutual funds, municipal bonds and variable annu-
             ities are complementary investments. Affluent investors
             should consider all three. Municipal bonds offer com-
             petitive current income and immediate liquidity. Vari-
             able annuities offer long-term growth and liquidity
             options. However, don't forget, like equities, municipal
             bonds are also subject to market risk and can lose value
             when interest rates increase.

Statement: "As a retired person, I can't afford to risk my money."

Response: The biggest investor risk, retired or not, is the loss of
             purchasing power (inflation), not losing money in a
             long-term, professionally managed investment (mar-
             ket risk). Variable annuities offer tax-deferred growth
             that provides the opportunity for long-term wealth
             accumulation.

Statement: "The fees are too high."

Response: Like Rodney Dangerfield's response to the question,
             "How's your wife?"—compared to what? Sophisticated
             and knowledgeable investors agree that there is no free
             lunch and an investor must pay for value. For the fees,
             an investor receives tax-deferred growth, professional
             management, control over tax payments, a guaranteed
             death benefit, freedom from probate, competitive long-
             term investment returns, and numerous distribution
             and settlement options.

Statement: "I am concerned about getting my money in an emer-
             gency." (A question of liquidity.)

Response: While withdrawals might be subject to penalties and
             taxes, investors can always get to their money. More

likely, investors will systematically withdraw their money over a period of time. An annuity has numerous options to meet those needs. For example, after the first year, the annuity allows an annual withdrawal of 10%, or you can withdraw the total accumulated earnings any time after the first year.

Also, once the contingent deferred sales charge period has passed, no withdrawal penalties are assessed. After age 59 1/2 no IRS penalties are assessed. Finally, IRS provisions usually allow withdrawals without penalty for permanent disability and other major adverse circumstances.

Statement: "I'm scared of the stock market and market risk."

Response: Investors of different ages have different fears. Investors 60 and older remember the effects of the 1929 stock market crash on their families and friends and are not very comfortable in the market regardless. Yuppies approaching 50 are usually not comfortable unless they are in the market. The yuppie fear is probably the higher risk of aggressive growth versus blue-chip, conservative growth.

In either case, for both groups, the real short-term fear is loss of investment capital. If an annuity were a short-term trading investment, their concerns would be reasonable. However, we are talking about long-term investing through the use of asset allocation. Over the long term, common stocks have always outperformed all other types of investments. That includes government bonds, CDs, municipal bonds, and corporate bonds. Also, market risk dissipates over time.

Again, investors must realize that the biggest long-term risk they face is inflation risk, not market risk. Market risk dissipates over time, inflation increases every year.

Question: "Why should I buy a variable annuity? I am already doing well with my investments."

Answer: A variable annuity is one building block of a financial plan, not the entire plan. It will contribute to an investor's overall goal of financial independence. Annuities complement other investments by offering additional diversification, competitive returns, and long-term tax-deferred growth.

Question: "I am a sophisticated investor making my own investment decisions. Why should I pay a sales commission to a representative?"

Answer: Variable annuities are securities. Representatives must be both insurance- and securities-licensed to sell variable annuities. A sales commission is paid to a representative whether or not his services are fully utilized, unless an investor purchases a no-load annuity. Since a commission will be paid, why not take full advantage of the representative's advisory talents?

Remember, there is no initial commission or up-front sales load paid on the purchase of an annuity. One hundred percent of an investor's money goes to work immediately. Also, annuities are long-term investments. Penalties for early withdrawal do not concern the long-term investor.

Purchasing a no-load annuity does have its advantages. There is no surrender penalty to consider. The fees are lower. The disadvantages are the limited number of no-load variable annuities available and that the investor is responsible for all investment reallocation decisions and monitoring the annual returns of the sub-account.

Question: "What are variable annuity sub-accounts?"

Answer: Sub-accounts are basically mutual funds with an advantage. The basic difference is that sub-account gains accumulate tax-deferred and re-allocating assets does not create a taxable event. All sub-account investing is done at net asset value (NAV). No commissions are charged.

As with mutual funds, numerous investment opportunities are available in the asset classes of stocks, bonds, and money markets. When selecting a variable annuity, an investor must consider the number of equity sub-accounts available. Equities outperform fixed-income securities over the long term.

Question: "Should I buy a fixed or a variable annuity?"

Answer: It depends. In either case, long-term wealth accumulation is the goal. If an investor invests for at least 10 years, a variable annuity is the better overall choice. However, if you have a specific financial goal in mind that requires performance predictability, a fixed annuity may be more appropriate.

Another approach is to purchase both a fixed and a variable annuity. This could be an excellent strategy, particularly if a fixed annuity can be purchased that offers a very competitive rate for a number of years (say 7% guaranteed for five years).

The general rule: over the longer term, the variable annuity is the better investment. The "comfort" of guaranteed fixed-income investment returns can be very expensive.

Statement: "The market is too high (too volatile)."

Response: Assume the investor is correct. Is the concern over short-term performance really important over the long-term? While the market will always have short-term fluctuations, the long-term market direction has always been up, and over the long term stocks have always outperformed other types of investments. Also remember that bonds can quickly sink in a high-interest environment.

Question: "Which sub-account(s) should I choose?"

Answer: It depends on an investor's goals and attitude toward risk. For a slightly aggressive long-term portfolio, 60% stocks, 40% bonds is a reasonable mix. More conservative investors may prefer an equally divided equities/fixed-income allocation. For 10-year investment time horizons, a 70% plus commitment may be appropriate for an affluent and diversified investor.

             Long-term allocation should favor equities. The exception is an investor who will retire within two years and use the assets to fund retirement. In this case, a conservative mix favoring fixed income becomes more appropriate.

Statement: "I could lose all my money in the market."

Response: Think about it logically. An investor invests in well-diversified, professionally managed sub-accounts containing quality securities. Without question, there is a short-term market risk. However, over the long term, the market direction has always been up and equities have always outperformed other investments. An investor's real risk is inflation. Variable annuities offer the opportunity for long-term wealth accumulation and address the risk of inflation.

Question: "What if I have a medical emergency?"

Answer: This is a legitimate concern for annuity investors. Most are 50 or older and are concerned about meeting financial emergencies, medical and otherwise.

Let's talk about the worst-case scenario. While early withdrawal and tax penalties might apply, an investor's money is still available. An investor under 59 1/2 would be subject to an additional 10% IRS tax. (For total disability, this penalty is generally waived.) There could be other penalties, depending on the terms of the contract. The income is taxed at ordinary income rates. An investor over 59 1/2 would be subject only to early withdrawal penalties. The income is taxed at ordinary income rates.

The more likely scenario will be as follows:

- Health emergencies will not develop.
- If they do, it will be after age 59 1/2.
- If they do, the CDSC requirements will have already been satisfied.

The probable result is that the distributed gains will be taxed at ordinary income tax rates. The returned contributions will not be taxed.

Statement: "I can't take a chance in the market with this money. If something happens to me, I want my spouse to receive it."

Response: An investor's beneficiary will always receive 100% of the contributions or the value of the contract, less withdrawals, whichever is greater. The guarantee is more of a comfort than a major benefit, but it is reassuring for spouses concerned about risk.

Question: "What is asset allocation?"

Answer: It is a more sophisticated way to diversify assets and reduce risk to achieve more competitive and consistent returns. It is one of the outstanding opportunities offered by a variable annuity.

              There are three areas for asset allocation: stocks, bonds, and cash. Within those categories are opportunities for further diversification. Take equities: an investor can choose between aggressive growth, growth, blue-chip, and balanced equity sub-accounts.

Question: "What about the taxes on the annuity?"

Answer: That's a great feature of an annuity. An investor has complete control over when the taxes will be paid.

              Until the money is withdrawn, no taxes are due. Partial withdrawals are taxed at ordinary income rates until all the earnings are dissipated. The total contributions are returned tax-free. An investor can actually delay paying taxes during his or her entire lifetime. Remember, until the money is withdrawn no taxes are due. Unlike tax-advantaged retirement plans like IRAs, there is no age limit for requiring distributions. (IRAs require distributions to start at 70 1/2.)

Statement: "I don't want to jeopardize my Social Security."

Response: Unless the assets are withdrawn, the growth remains tax-deferred and has absolutely no effect on your Social

Security inclusion calculations or monthly benefits. The assets continue to grow untaxed and uncounted until withdrawals commence.

Question: "How does an annuity avoid probate?"

Answer: At the contract owner's death, the annuity value (the value is never less than the contributions, less the withdrawals), passes directly to the beneficiary. It offers the beneficiary instant liquidity and no delays.

Question: "What about estate taxes?"

Answer: If the contract owner dies during the deferral period, the value is included for purposes of determining estate taxes. If the contract owner has annuitized and the payments continue to a beneficiary, the present value of future payments is included in the estate calculations.

Statement: "I need guaranteed income when I retire."

Response: If annuitized, variable annuities can offer either a guaranteed or variable return. An investor also has other options, including personally designing a program that includes systematic withdrawals or a lump-sum distribution. (This author does not recommend annuitization.)

Question: "Why do I pay mortality and expense charges?"

Answer: Mortality charges guarantee that the beneficiary, at the death of the contract owner, will receive the greater of the total contributions or the account value, less withdrawals. The expense charges pay administration costs.

Question: "What commissions must I pay for buying the subaccounts?"

Answer: You pay no commissions. All annuity units (shares) are
             purchased at net asset value (NAV).

Question: "Who manages the money invested in the sub-ac-
             counts?"

Answer: The insurance company is responsible for managing
             the sub-accounts' assets. The assets are managed either
             by internal managers, outside advisors, or a combina-
             tion of both.

Question: "What happens if the market crashes?"

Answer: The value of the sub-accounts will decline. To reiterate:
             An annuity is a long-term investment; short-term risk
             dissipates over time; and, over the long term, a well -
             anaged equity portfolio has always appreciated in value
             despite crashes, high interest rates, and everything else
             that causes market concern.

Question: "How much can I contribute to an annuity?"

             Answer: There are no limitations on how much you can
             invest. Without prior approval, insurance companies
             may place certain maximum limits (usually $5000,000
             or more) on contributions.

             Annuities differ from retirement plans in the following
             manner:

             • Annuity contributions are not tax deductible nor are
               the contributions limited. Retirement plan contribu-
               tions are limited but deductible.
             • Retirement plans have distribution requirements
               based on attaining a certain age. Variable annuities
               have no distribution requirements based on age or
               other factors except death of the contract owner.

Note: retirement plans and variable annuities accumulate wealth tax-deferred.

Question: "What would you do if you were me?"

Answer: Of all the investor questions asked, this is the most commonly heard by investment advisors. Presenting an advisor's perspective may help investors better understand their own investment needs.

From this advisor's viewpoint, before considering the purchase of a variable annuity, or any other type of investment, investors should have a clear understanding of their long-term objectives, time horizon, current asset mix, tolerance for risk, approximate net worth, and a researched decision that a variable annuity is both suitable and the best use of long-term investment assets.

Succinctly expressed: being a knowledgeable, informed investor will improve your chances of success by 1,000 percent. Informed investors are the advisor's dream clients.

Summary

- Variable annuity investors have seven primary areas of concern: stock market risk, sub-account performance, fees, liquidity, personal income taxes, the long-term investment commitment, and safety.
- Most annuity investors are 50 or older. Many are retired or planning for retirement in the near future. Their major investment concern is preservation of capital, as they usually underestimate their life expectancy by several years.
- Many 50-plus investors prefer CDs and other guaranteed investments because of their perceived safety. While safe from

market fluctuations, CDs do not address the real risk of investing: not maintaining purchasing power to conquer the devastating effects of inflation.

- Variable annuities' fees are higher than most mutual funds but they offer the added advantage of tax-deferred wealth accumulation.

- Long-term market risk is dissipated by diversification and time. Older investors prefer a less aggressive investment strategy. The younger "yuppie" generation usually prefers a more aggressive risk strategy. Both should realize that the real risk is inflation.

- The choice between purchasing a variable or fixed annuity depends on an investor's time horizon, risk tolerance, and investment objectives. For time horizons of 10 or more years, variable annuities are the best choice.

- Short-term risk is a concern but not a significant factor in long-term investing. Time dissipates risk, and performance becomes more consistent as the time horizon expands.

- Annuity assets are reasonably available. While penalties and taxes could apply, the money can be disbursed immediately.

- Variable annuities allow investors to have control over the timing of the payment of their variable annuity income taxes. There are no age requirements on when variable annuity assets must be disbursed.

- There are no contribution limitations on annuity purchases. The contributions are also not tax-deductible.

- Knowledgeable and informed investors have a 1,000 percent better chance of investing successfully.

12

COMMONSENSE INVESTING AND VARIABLE ANNUITIES

KEY CONCEPTS

▼ Understanding Realistic Investment Goals

▼ The Three Absolute "Don'ts" of Investing

▼ Implementing Successful Investment Strategies

▼ Monitoring the Total Return Results

As an investor you find tax-deferred wealth accumulation an attractive opportunity. Your financial circumstances are positive. You plan to continue working another 10 years. You can invest $10,000 annually toward your retirement. Your choices are your company's 401(k) plan or a self-funded variable annuity. You hesitate to invest in the 401(k) because you might accept an employment offer from another company in six months. What would be a commonsense decision?

There are seldom absolute investment solutions. Nevertheless, the choice in the above scenario is fairly clear. The 401(k) contri-

butions are deductible—this reduces current tax liabilities. Employers often contribute to an employee's retirement plan. Even if an
employee leaves, the contributions can remain and grow tax-
deferred. If not, the assets can be rolled over to an IRA. Common
sense gives you the answer.

Regrettably, the choices are rarely so clearly defined.

As an investment advisor, my client conferences include an in-
depth discussion on practical investing and realistic investment expectations. Many otherwise sophisticated clients have unrealistic expectations about financial goals and investment returns. This is particularly true of CD savers and inexperienced investors seeking the perfect,
no-risk/high-return investment. Understanding what to expect, both
positively and negatively, is essential to successful long-term investing.
It is also important for the emotional comfort of an investor.

There are two distinct, complementary, and comprehensive disciplines involved in commonsense investing: quantitative and qualitative. One is measurable and one is subjective. Quantitative commonsense investing deals with selecting investments through the use
of research and analysis. A qualitative approach includes an analysis
of the investor's financial goals, investment preferences, and investment judgment.

When is the purchase of an annuity appropriate? The short
answer is when it is suitable and the best alternative. The chances of
making the correct decision are enhanced when the annuity's risks
and rewards are clearly understood.

One Dozen Commonsense
Investing Strategies

Experienced and inexperienced investors alike will benefit from a
review of the basics. For advanced investors it is a reality check. For
less experienced, but equally bright and willing to learn, investors it

can be a blueprint for both investment success and the elimination of sub-par investment decisions.

"Get Real" Investing

There are three investment "get real" situations that must be avoided at all costs:

1. Avoid investment recommendations that promise unrealistic returns. All successful investors have a common trait—realistic expectations. For example, equity mutual fund and sub-account investors anticipating an average 10%, 10-year, annualized return have realistic expectations. Realistic, not guaranteed. Investors anticipating a 10-year, 20% annualized equity return are optimistic, but not particularly realistic.

Overly optimistic statements made by inexperienced, ill-informed, or dishonest sales representatives should confirm immediately that something is amiss. Also, misrepresentation is not confined to the securities industry. It also includes areas such as real estate, fine arts, antiques, coins, and stamps. "Let the buyer beware!" is always appropriate advice before you write a check.

Fortunately the investment and insurance industries are well regulated, well monitored, and require training, testing, and extensive background checks before a sales representative can become licensed to sell either insurance or securities.

Caveat: Most securities misrepresentations are outside the industry. Unlicensed individuals selling unregistered securities and confidence schemes are the biggest problems. Each is illegal. Involvement can be avoided by asking two direct questions: Who is this person? and Is what he's telling me realistic?

2. Never purchase a security on a cold call from someone you don't know—never. Always know with whom you are dealing.

Imagine this scenario. "You send me a check for $10,000 and you can get in on a really good deal. You won't receive a prospectus, but don't worry. You really don't need to know anything about the deal to make money. We've never met but that's okay. Trust me, I work on Wall Street. Besides, customers who invest in our [choose one: commodities, gold, metals, fine arts, heating oil, penny stocks] often double their money within three to six months."

Would you send a $10,000 check to this person? It is amazing how many otherwise intelligent individuals send huge sums to people they have never met in cities hundreds of miles away. As you might imagine, this isn't a recommended approach to wealth accumulation (unless you are the salesperson).

3. Never buy a "hot tip" unless you can afford to lose most or all of the money invested.

Here's another scenario. "You have been chosen over the mavens of Wall Street to participate in a really great new-issue deal." Get real! Hot stock issues are almost always sold to institutions or affluent individuals with established working relationships with the selling firm.

The best "get real" advice is to never purchase a security on a hot tip. Remember, your investment goal is long-term wealth accumulation, not get-rich-quick schemes.

Our initial three commonsense investing recommendations deal primarily with the honesty, integrity, and intentions of the sales representative. Succinctly, an investor should deal with a financial advisor and a financial institution whom he or she trusts. Always avoid "hot deals" and unrealistic expectations.

Our next segment presents some commonsense strategies that can be implemented by the investor. Becoming a proactive investor will not only bring you happy trails, but can also dramatically improve your financial picture.

4. Stop procrastinating: commit to a well-designed and well executed long-term financial plan.

It has often been said that most individuals spend more time planning their vacation than their financial future. Procrastination is expensive. Investor inaction results from lack of investment knowledge and an unrealistic concern for the loss of capital. By purchasing short-term investments to meet long-term financial goals, investors exacerbate the problem. While committing to a formalized investment plan may not be easy, it is absolutely necessary if you are serious about wealth accumulation.

5. Monitoring your investments can dramatically increase their total return. There is a real difference between long-term investing and lifetime investing. Successful investors purchase quality investments and keep them for an extended period. This is quite different from the buy-and-die strategy: put your assets in a safe-deposit box for the heirs. Fortunately, investors in variable annuities and mutual funds have employed money managers to make the securities reallocation decisions.

While investors purchase mutual funds and annuities as long-term investments, a periodic review is important to confirm their suitability and performance and to evaluate an overall financial strategy. Sometimes it is appropriate to sell, rebalance, or reallocate assets to increase returns, reduce risk, or meet changing market conditions. Variable annuities are well suited for maintaining a desired asset-allocation mix, as switching between sub-accounts does not create taxable events.

6. Understanding bond market risk and return will improve investment strategies and increase net returns. Savers purchasing CDs understand that the rate is guaranteed for a certain period. At maturity, the saver receives back 100% of the invested principal and the interest due. Savers expanding their investment horizons often assume the same guarantees are in force for the bond market. This can be a costly assumption.

U.S. government securities may have no credit risk but they do have market risk. Corporate bonds have both market risk and credit risk. As interest rates rise, bond prices decline. Conversely, as interest rates decline, bond prices rise.

Many mutual fund and sub-account investors assume that when interest rates rise they receive higher returns. That is correct. That is the good news. The bad news is that fixed-income investments decline in value when rates rise. Hence, investors must consider the mutual fund or variable annuity sub-account's total return, not just its current yield. For example, say a high-yield corporate bond sub-account paid a 9.2% yield for one year. An investor received $920 in interest from a $10,000 investment. Interest rates increased dramatically during the year. The sub-account's investment unit price decreased in value by 5%. The net annual return is 4.2%, not 9.2%:

9.2% (interest) +/− (price difference) − 5% = 4.2% net

Confusion arises when the definition of a "guarantee" is not clearly understood by an investor. With government bonds, only the return of principal at maturity is guaranteed. The misunderstanding arises because the bonds, unlike CDs, are not guaranteed against market losses, which can be dramatic.

In the author's opinion, the biggest mistake fixed-income investors make is seeking the highest current yield while ignoring quality. Again, CD buyers assume that their money will be returned at maturity regardless: wrong! This is another major reason why hiring professional money managers is so important.

Bond prices are affected by the interest-rate environment, the bond's quality, and its maturity date. A variable annuity fixed-income sub-account's investment unit value will fluctuate with changing market conditions. Again, the interest rate, return of principal, and ratings quality are not guaranteed.

7. Purchasing tax-advantaged investments is not always a great idea.

Investors have two readily available opportunities for tax-deferred wealth accumulation: retirement plans and annuities. An additional tax-advantaged opportunity for tax-free income exists with municipal bonds. The ideal strategy is to receive competitive returns and defer or eliminate tax obligations.

When should an investor purchase a tax-advantaged investment? The commonsense answer is, only when it makes economic sense— not when the only motive is saving taxes. After all the smoke clears, the question is, What is the investment's bottom line? Is it more beneficial than other investment alternatives?

For working individuals able to contribute to a qualified retirement plan, participation should be a given. The contributions are deductible and the money grows tax-deferred. Retired individuals should consider a rollover of their retirement assets to continue the tax-deferred growth even if they need some assets for income. Affluent investors should also consider tax-free income and tax-deferred wealth accumulation. Retirement plans, municipal bonds, and annuities can be the foundation for a very prosperous plan. However, tax-advantaged investments are not always the most appropriate choice and are not always properly positioned by investors.

Everyone agrees that investing in a retirement plan is a reasonable and prudent approach to wealth accumulation. What is not appropriate is placing municipal bonds in a retirement account. Municipal bond yields are lower than comparable quality corporate bonds, and the retirement plan income is already tax-deferred. When the tax-free income is paid out of the retirement plan, it will be taxable income. It makes absolutely no sense to receive a lower yield and then pay taxes on previously tax-free income.

Purchasing municipal bonds when an investor is taxed at 15% is probably not a good idea as the tax advantages usually don't offset the lower tax-free yields. Also remember that most states collecting income taxes tax municipal bond income, although most states make exceptions for in-state bonds. Even the most affluent investors have some of their income taxed at 15%. There is a place for corporate bond mutual funds in everyone's fixed-income investment portfolio. (See Table 12–1.)

Using an annuity as an investment vehicle for a retirement plan is also a questionable practice in the opinion of this author. The income is already tax-deferred. It will remain taxable upon distribution. The investor does receive certain insurance benefits (i.e., guaranteed death benefits) but high annuity mortality and expense charges can adversely affect the annuity's overall performance.

Often the question arises as to whether a mutual fund or a variable annuity is the more appropriate investment. It depends on the circumstances.

If an investor's capital appreciation and income from mutual fund investments will be taxed at 15%, if an investor's time horizon is five years or less, or if significant or total liquidity is an issue, mutual funds are usually more appropriate. Variable annuities are most appropriate for providing long-term wealth accumulation and tax deferral in a total investment strategy. They are also an outstanding alternative to retirement plans for continuing tax-deferred growth after age 70 1/2.

Table 12–1. Tax Effects on Municipal Bond and Corporate Bond Income

Example:

	Municipal Bond Fund		Corporate Bond Fund	
	Rate	Interest	Rate	Interest
Income	6.5%	$65	8%	$80
15% Income Tax				(12)
Net Income		$65		$68

---

8. Proven investment techniques provide more performance consistency and more competitive returns.

Having a degree in accounting does not preclude an investor from employing a CPA to complete an income tax return. Being knowledgeable about money management does not preclude an investor, or an advisor for that matter, from employing a professional money manager. The goal is to select the best talent available and take advantage of those talents.

The primary "job" of a mutual fund and variable annuity investor is to select the best asset manager, not personally select individual securities. Often financial advisors assist in the manager selection process. Once selected, the asset managers manage the money. Selecting the asset managers is the first step in building wealth, not the final step.

An extremely important method for providing consistent and competitive returns is asset allocation. Equities should be the best performing asset class over a long period; thus, an investor may wish to allocate a larger portion of the sub-account assets (50 to 80%) to equities during the early years. Within that allocation a portion should include aggressive growth and foreign securities. However, the major emphasis should be on high-quality equities.

Another important investment consideration is patience. A real investment "skill" is simply leaving money invested in quality investments over a number of years and allowing them to grow. The combination of time, quality, and compounding make investment gurus out of the most humble investors.

Total return investing is important to wealth accumulation. The bottom line or total return is the net amount earned during a given period, usually measured annually. The reason for asset allocation and diversification is not only to reduce risk but also to receive competitive returns from the best-performing investment securities. In Table 12–2, the income investor seeking the highest current yield has the

Table 12–2. Examples of Total Return: Equity Sub-Accounts

	A	B	C
Stock Capital Appreciation	5%	15%	(3%)
Stock Dividend Yield	4%	-0-	7%
Total Return	9%	15%	4%

least desirable total return investment. Other considerations must still include quality, volatility, and risk.

9.   Define the difference between time and market timing.

The market timing thesis involves anticipating the direction of the market. The strategy: invest when the market is rising and withdraw from the market when it is declining. Great theory, but does it work in practice? To quote Will Rogers, "An economist is a man that can tell you what can happen under any condition, and his guess is liable to be as good as anybody else's, too." With due respect to some very bright individuals, for hundreds of years investors have tried to determine the short-term direction of the stock market to maximize profits. The success rate has been limited.

The "new" wisdom about market timing is that it is really not about maximizing profits but about controlling risk. The end result appears to be that while market timing can lessen the effect of market declines, it is counterbalanced by asset underperformance during rising markets. The bottom line? You may miss some of a bear market, but you will also miss an equal or larger portion of a bull market. Another problem with market timing is that trading securities outside sheltered vehicles, like qualified plans and variable annuity sub-accounts, generates immediate taxable events and increases commissions and other charges.

Many commonsense investment strategies are more appropriate and potentially more profitable than market timing. The first recommendation is our quality-plus-time formula. Purchase a number of quality equity mutual funds and hold them for a long period of time. Simple yet effective. Investing in a variable annuity and allocating your assets to equity sub-accounts will accomplish the same goal.

A risk-reduction strategy can be further enhanced by using dollar-cost averaging, asset allocation, and diversification. Investors continue to seek alternatives to quality plus time plus compounding. Hope springs eternal. The long-term results favor $(Q + T + C)$ until something better hits Wall Street. Of course it has only been 200 years.

10. Determining acceptable risk by using commitment, temperament, and time horizon. These three strategic parameters dictate the initial and subsequent decisions on variable annuity investing. The initial investment screens should evaluate whether the available assets can be invested for seven or more years; whether the investor's temperament will accept market risk; and whether the investor will devote sufficient time to monitoring the variable annuity sub-accounts. If the response to any one of the three screens is negative, a variable annuity is not an appropriate investment choice.

Assuming a positive response, the guidelines are as stated. A long-term commitment is essential to allow tax-deferred growth through compounding. A second consideration is sufficient time to eliminate the possibility of contingent deferred sales charges (CDSC).

Market risk assumption is necessary to receive competitive returns and outpace inflation. The strategy must include a commitment to investing in diversified equities. Balanced equity/bond sub-accounts are also acceptable. The equities are part of an asset allocation model that includes fixed-income and money market sub-accounts.

Our third screen requires investor commitment. The investor consults an investment advisor. Together they make a purchasing decision. They hire outstanding sub-account managers by purchasing an annuity. So far, so good. However, one more ingredient is necessary—the periodic monitoring of the sub-accounts' overall long-term performance.

A favorite Texas adage is appropriate here: "Trust your neighbor, but brand your cattle." You trust the research, judgment, and integrity of your financial advisor. Regardless, successful investors are knowledgeable, informed, and capable of making asset allocation and risk decisions without outside assistance. Circumstances can change; financial advisors retire, leave the business, or relocate. Therefore, investors should be prepared to manage their own assets.

11. Choosing an insurance company when purchasing a variable or fixed annuity.

There is one absolute rule recommended: invest your money with an insurance company that carries a quality rating determined by services such as A. M. Best, Standard & Poor's, and Moody's. Given a choice, the assurance of safety is worth receiving a smaller return.

An investor's variable annuity assets are guaranteed by an insurance company's full faith and credit. The assets are held in trust by a custodian—a double safety net of protection. A fixed annuity is guaranteed by the company's full faith and credit and the assets of the general account.

Prior to purchase, an investor should review the asset mix of the insurance company's general account. This is available from their sales literature and/or regulatory filings, or ask the sales representative for the information. The portfolio diversification indicates the company's investment strategy and approach to risk. This is particularly important for fixed annuity investors. The general account assures the safety and performance of the fixed annuity. General account investment practices are dictated by state insurance commissions. Legal reserve requirements are established by state laws that direct insurance companies to set aside sufficient assets to indemnify their policyholders for future contract claims.

The reserve allocations are based upon mortality tables and interest-rate assumptions dictated by statute. The reserve assets must be invested in high-quality securities, usually fixed-income. Excess asset reserves may be invested in lower-quality investments, including high-yield bonds. Thus, the solvency of an insurance company can be adversely affected by its investment policies.

While safety and performance are the important considerations when selecting an insurance company, other factors must also be considered. Obviously the contract structure is important. This includes fees, deferred sales charges, sub-accounts, and other features and benefits. You must also consider the local and home office service policy, as services vary widely. Determine the range and quality of services available before you purchase an annuity.

12. Quantitative (measurable) analysis for the average investor.

Now that you are a brilliant investor, it is time to learn the methods for measuring your success. It is a challenge for investors to determine how well they are doing—really doing. However, the problem can be solved very effectively and efficiently.

There are two methods for determining performance. The first is to become an analyst and review the prospectus and state filings for performance, fees, features, benefits, and other pedestrian information. The other is to use various research publications. My recommendation? Research publications. My preferred sources for quick and easy performance, ranking, and risk valuations are Value Line and Morningstar. Their addresses are listed in the sources section of this book.

An investor's "job" is not to be an analyst. Rather, it is to become a knowledgeable individual seeking the most efficient method for evaluating investments. Research services are fast, accurate, comprehensive, and affordable.

Summary

- Common sense should dictate when and when not to invest in variable annuities. A variable annuity can be an excellent investment and a significant contributor to a well-designed, well-diversified investment strategy.
- Chances for investment success are greatly enhanced when investors have a realistic understanding of investment expectations. This is particularly true of CD savers and inexperienced investors seeking a perfect no-risk/high-return investment. It doesn't exist.
- There are two complementary and comprehensive investment disciplines in commonsense investing: quantitative and qualitative. One is measurable and one is subjective.
- "Get real" investing demands that an investor analyze an investment opportunity to determine if the performance expectations are realistic and the sales representative honest. The worst mistake investors make is buying securities from inexperienced, ill-informed, or dishonest sales representatives. There are three absolutes in "get real" investing: avoid unrealistic return promises, never purchase a security on a cold call, and never buy a "hot tip."
- Procrastination is an expensive habit. Investors should commit to a well-designed and well-executed financial plan. Proactive investing reduces undue concern for capital preservation and it eliminates using short-term investments to meet long-term financial goals.
- There is a difference between credit risk and market risk. When interest rates rise, bond prices decline. Conversely, as interest rates decline, bond prices rise. This is an elementary fact of the bond market, but a most important fact to remember.

- Purchasing the highest yield and ignoring total return and investment quality is a common error of inexperienced investors. Total return (bottom line) investing is the true measure of successful investing.
- There are proven investment techniques that have always been successful. Despite much effort to change the system, the best investment approach remains quality investments + time + compounding (Q + T + C).
- There is a difference between market timing and time when investing: one works. Market timing may reduce risk, but it also reduces investment return. Market timing can also create taxable events for nonsheltered investments by "trading" the market.
- Commonsense investing can determine acceptable risk by using an approach that includes temperament, time horizon, and investor commitment.
- Now that you have become a brilliant variable annuity investor you should measure your success. The quick and easy method is to use research publications.

13

COMPARING VARIABLE ANNUITIES AND OTHER INVESTMENTS

KEY CONCEPTS

▼ Home Ownership Advantages

▼ Variable Annuities and Mutual Funds

▼ Life Insurance as an Investment

▼ Combining Fixed Annuities and Government Securities

The purchase of a variable annuity is most beneficial as part of a comprehensive, well-designed, and appropriately executed long-term financial plan. Many investors blend variable annuities with retirement plans, municipal bonds, mutual funds, and equities to form the bedrock of a complete tax-advantaged retirement and wealth-accumulation strategy. Although our emphasis has been on the tax-deferred and tax-advantaged approach to reaching financial goals and objectives, a complete investment strategy also includes other assets and securities. One important area is real estate.

Without question, the purchase of a home is an important part of an investment program. Besides the pride of ownership and the sense of security, the purchase of a primary residence offers an opportunity for tax advantages, long-term capital gains, and deferred wealth accumulation. During the period of ownership, mortgage interest payments and local and state property taxes are deductible. The annual tax savings are in direct correlation to a homeowner's maximum marginal tax rate. (See Table 13–1.)

Homeowners build tax-deferred equity with every mortgage payment and with the appreciation in value of the home. No taxes are

---

Table 13–1

Example: A homeowner whose top marginal tax rate is 28% makes a $15,000 annual mortgage and a $3,000 annual property tax payment.

Total Annual Mortgage Payment	$15,000
Credited to Reducing Loan	($2,000)
Total Mortgage Interest Paid	$13,000
Total Property Taxes	$3,000
Interest and Taxes Paid	$16,000
28% of $13,000 (Mortgage)	($3,640)
28% of $ 3,000 (Taxes)	($840)
Net Annual Cost of Owning Home	$11,520

Note: If an owner of a $150,000 home assumes an annual price appreciation equal to a 4% inflation rate, the results are even more impressive.

Net Annual Cost of Owning Home	$11,520
4% Annual Price Appreciation	($6,000)
Net-Net Annual Cost	$5,520
Net Monthly Cost $5,520/12	$460

due or gains recognized until the home is sold. Even if the home is sold, the gain can be deferred by purchasing another home of equal or greater value within two years of the sale date. After age 55, a homeowner may elect to exercise a once-in-a-lifetime exemption on the sale of a primary residence and not pay taxes on a substantial portion of the long-term capital gains. The present maximum long-term capital gains exclusion is $125,000 (see Table 13–2).

Caveat: a 55-year-old or older homeowner seeking an exclusion should consult a tax professional before the sale. Restrictions may apply, particularly for couples over 55, both owning homes and seeking to remarry.

The purchase of a primary residence is usually more important than any other type of investment for an individual. While the capital appreciation of a residence is not assured, it is still the best long-term investment for most individuals and families. However, there are disadvantages to investing in real estate. Until the mid-1980s, home ownership was the foundation for wealth accumulation for most families. Most homes increased in value each year. However, during the mid-1980s, a period of deflation and recession, many

Table 13–2

Example: Home Sale of a Primary Residence Owner over 55

Sale Price of Home	$250,000
Cost Basis of Home	$60,000
Long-Term Capital Gains (L.T.C.G.) on Sale	$190,000
One-Time Exemption	($125,000)
Long-Term Capital Gains (L.T.C.G.) Tax Due on Balance	$65,000
Taxes on $ 65,000 @ 28%	$18,200
versus	
Taxes on $190,000 @ 28%	$53,200

homeowners experienced something startling: their home's value decreased. In areas like the Northeast and the West Coast values dropped dramatically.

During this period, the commercial real estate market fared even worse. Many developers, lenders, and investors were literally forced into bankruptcy because of the falling real estate prices, excessive development, and high mortgage rates. Fortunately, home values in the mid-1990s have firmed. Once again homes and commercial real estate are appreciating in price, although much more modestly than in past years.

Another disadvantage of real estate investing is lack of liquidity. Unlike securities, home sales are complicated, expensive, time-consuming, and require extended periods of time to consummate. Commercial properties are even more illiquid, and their sales are certainly more complicated.

Finally, investors must be careful about diversification. A disproportionate percentage of their assets should not be committed to real estate. This is particularly true when leverage (borrowing money) is used to purchase real estate. Regardless, investors should always give strong consideration and preference to purchasing a home.

Another group of investments that should be given strong consideration for building wealth is mutual funds. If you already own a variable annuity, you probably already own mutual funds. Variable annuity owners certainly invest in sub-accounts, the mutual fund equivalent "wrapped" in an insurance contract. So, why not invest in mutual funds in conjunction with variable annuities?

Annuities Versus Mutual Funds

Mutual funds and annuities are the vehicles of choice for millions of investors. Each offers access to professional money management, long-term competitive returns, flexibility, and liquidity. Annuities and mutual funds also have certain benefits and limitations that are individually unique.

Mutual funds and annuities share the following benefits:

Professional Money Management: The assets are managed by the most qualified and successful money managers available. They offer access to institutional management, competitive and consistent returns, and assurance that the assets are managed by experts.

Flexibility: Each offers numerous investment choices. Investors can choose investments that meet their present investment objectives and reallocate their assets when their investment objectives change.

Regulation: Each is highly regulated by both federal and state statutes. Requirements include providing a prospectus, periodic reporting, full disclosure, antifraud rules, and meeting certain operating standards. Mutual funds and variable annuities are classified as securities and are regulated by the Securities and Exchange Commission. State insurance and securities commissions also regulate certain activities of the mutual fund companies and insurance companies sponsoring variable and fixed annuities and their agents and representatives.

Accessibility: Annuities and mutual funds are easy to buy. Both are sold through various channels of distribution including stock brokers, insurance agents, bank representatives, and direct marketing groups. (Annuity sales by banks are restricted in some states.) Nominal initial and subsequent purchase minimums are also common to both investments.

Paperwork and Record Keeping: Each is required to provide extensive reporting to both investors and regulatory agencies, including the SEC and various states in which the investments are sold.

Daily Record of Performance: Each is required to evaluate the value of their shares (accumulation units) daily. Mutual fund prices are published in daily financial publications, larger daily newspapers, and most investment periodicals. Annuity prices are more often published in general and specialized investment publications on a weekly basis.

Diversification: Both offer sufficient investment choices to reduce risk, design an appropriate portfolio, and reallocate assets should an investment objective change or a reallocation be necessary to rebalance a portfolio.

Inflation Hedge: The bedrock defense against inflation is investing in nonguaranteed securities that offer the potential for growth in excess of the annual inflation rate (CPI). Variable annuities and mutual funds that offer equities (stocks) in their sub-accounts (funds) provide a defense against inflation.

Significant Differences Between Mutual Funds and Annuities

Taxation

Mutual funds are:

- Subject to current taxation on any realized capital gain or dividend distribution.
- Subject to taxation of any gains realized from the sale of assets (shares).

Annuities are not:

- Subject to current taxation on any realized capital gain or dividend distribution.
- Subject to taxation on any gains realized from the reallocation of assets within the framework of the annuity (sub-account switch).

Investment Note: Annuity payments in excess of the tax-free investment return are taxed at ordinary income rates when distributed. This includes capital gains and assumes annuitization.

Tax-Deferred Annuity Wealth Accumulation

Both variable and fixed annuities are long-term investments. The most important advantage of an annuity versus a mutual fund is that annuity assets compound tax-deferred.

1. The reallocation of assets is not a taxable event (variable annuity).
2. The contributions, account appreciation, and assets retained that would otherwise be paid in taxes are allowed to grow tax-deferred.
3. Taxes are not due on accumulated assets until distributed.

Fees and Expenses

Annuity fees are more expensive than their mutual funds counterparts because of the mortality (insurance) charge, which provides insurance coverage for the annuity owner. At the annuitant's death, the beneficiary receives the value of the fixed/sub-account(s) or the value of the investment contributions, less withdrawals, whichever is greater.

Liquidity

Mutual fund owners have immediate and unrestricted access to their assets. The mutual fund sponsor stands ready to partially or fully redeem an investor's shares. The price may be more or less than the original cost. Current share prices are calculated daily. Mutual funds also offer systematic withdrawal plans and the distribution of capital gains and/or dividends as earned.

Investment Note: Mutual funds may be subject to early redemption charges if the investor purchased shares with a potential deferred sales charge ("B" shares and certain "C" shares).

Annuities also offer numerous distribution plans, including lump-sum, partial, and systematic distributions. However, as annuities are defined as long-term investments, they have more restrictive distribution rules, including:

1. Annuities can be subject to substantial withdrawal penalties during early contract years.
2. Annuities are subject to a 10% IRS penalty for withdrawals prior to the annuity owner reaching age 59 1/2.
3. Withdrawals in excess of stated limits, such as 10% per year or the accumulated earnings, can be subject to additional penalties.

Social Security and Annuities

A new, higher inclusion rate may increase the amount of Social Security benefits included in taxable income for retirees receiving Social Security benefits. Presently all annuity earnings are excluded from gross income calculations unless distributed.

Municipal Bonds and Annuities

Both municipal bonds and variable annuities offer investors tax advantages. Variable annuities offer tax-deferred wealth accumulation with capital appreciation. Municipal bonds offer fixed-rate, tax-free income. Both nonqualified annuities and municipal bonds are purchased with after-tax dollars. One is a short- to long-term income vehicle, the other is a long-term growth investment. Neither is a mutually exclusive investment opportunity. Most investors purchase municipal bonds prior to investing in an annuity to maintain liquidity and to receive tax-free income and competitive net yields. However, once a bond buyer seeks diversification, an annuity is a potential alternative.

Investors agree that both are excellent opportunities, depending on individual needs. One overriding question with a municipal bond buyer is the method of purchase. Should a bond buyer purchase individual issues or municipal bond mutual funds? The answer often depends on the amount of money involved. For less than $250,000 to $500,000 an investor is probably better served with mutual funds because of the professional management. Even with larger sums, unless a municipal bond investor is a tax-free fixed-income expert, he or she should consider either mutual funds or a professional fixed-income manager. Regardless, there is a place for both municipal bonds and variable annuities in a diversified portfolio.

Life Insurance

Life insurance is a simple concept. An individual purchases a contract from an insurance company, which promises to pay a beneficiary a specified amount when the insured person dies. For that promise, a predetermined sum (premium) is paid to the company. The primary purpose of insurance is to provide protection for the insured's family, business, or other defined risk. Insurance is an excellent method for providing liquidity at the time of the insured's death.

There are two major types of insurance: whole (ordinary) life and term life. Within those two classifications are numerous subtypes. Individuals purchase policies either individually or as part of an employee group.

Life insurance can be an efficient, effective method for transferring risk to the insurance company. It can guarantee an insured that, at his or her death, sufficient funds will be available to meet certain obligations such as taxes, estate liquidity, educating children, and paying off a mortgage. For our purposes, the question is, Is it a good investment?

A definitive answer is difficult until one understands an investment as it relates to insurance. Insurance is a great investment when the goal is protection, peace of mind, and funding needs at death.

When an ordinary life insurance policy is compared to a variable annuity as an investment the answer is that it is probably not so great. However, you are comparing two dissimilar types of policies. Life insurance is primarily for protection. Variable annuities are primarily for accumulating tax-deferred, long-term wealth.

From an investment perspective the question has always been, Does an investor purchase an ordinary policy or purchase a term policy and invest the premium savings? Based on pure economics, an investor needing protection is usually better served buying a term policy. A term policy provides pure protection. The policy pays the benefit only if the insured dies. Term is the cheapest form of protection. An insured can purchase substantially more coverage for the same premium versus ordinary life. The downside is that there is no accumulation of cash value. Is accumulating cash value better than buying pure protection and investing the difference? For a disciplined investor, the author's answer is no.

Term life insurance is purchased for a specified period of time. Policies with the most competitive initial rates are annual renewal term (ART). The cost of insurance increases each year. The coverage remains the same. Level term is purchased for specific periods, usually 5, 10, or 20 years. The premium remains level for the specified time period, but it is initially more expensive than ART. It is renewed at a higher rate at the initial guaranteed period's end. The coverage remains the same.

Another popular type of term insurance is decreasing term. The policy is sold in conjunction with a home mortgage. As the mortgage balance declines so does the insurance coverage. Its purpose is to pay off the mortgage balance should the insured die prior to the mortgage being retired.

The ordinary life policies sold until the late 1970s to early 1980s were not good investments. The cost of insurance was expensive, and the policy return guarantees ranged between 2 and 4%. Policies were sold as protection and as savings vehicles. With the introduction of universal life in 1979, the insurance business changed swiftly. The sales of universal life increased dramatically as the policies paid much higher returns than traditional ordinary life policies. Universal life policies are different in that there is separate accounting for insurance cost, expenses, and rates of return for the policies. The policies combine renewable term and an investment account. While universal life pays a higher investment return, the insurance cost is also generally higher. Again, since the primary function of life insurance is protection, a universal life policy's true insurance expense should be determined before purchase.

Finally, a universal variable life insurance policy can be purchased. The investments are placed in a separate account (i.e., stocks, bonds, and cash) which is similar to the variable annuity approach. The minimum death benefit is guaranteed and can increase. The premium remains constant. The investment returns depend on the underlying securities' performance.

The relationship between life insurance policies and variable annuity contracts is intricate but important. The purpose of insurance is protection. Purchasing pure coverage (term) and investing the difference will usually produce a better net return than purchasing a policy and combining insurance and investing. The savings can be invested in a variable annuity or other, more competitive investments.

It is important to note that the cost of insurance becomes more expensive each year of a person's life. The investment question arises, How much coverage does a policyholder really have in a policy? In evaluating Table 13–3, the question is, What is the cost of purchasing an annual renewal term policy for the 20 years of coverage? Assuming the difference is invested at a certain percentage, what would be the value of the account versus the cash value of the policy.

Table 13–3

An Example: An individual purchases a $100,000 whole life policy. The annual premium is $2,500.00. Purchaser is male age 35.

Policy Year	Cash Value	Premium Paid	Death Benefit
1	$150	$2,500	$100,000
5	$7000	$12,500	$100,000
10	$17,000	$25,000	$100,000
15	$27,000	$37,500	$100,000
20*	$37,200*	$50,000*	$100,000*

For illustration purposes only. Not actual data.

*Note that the pure insurance coverage after 20 years is $62,800 ($100,000 coverage – $37,200 cash value). At death the beneficiary receives the face value, not the face value and the cash value combined.

Again, this is an important decision, as the insurance purchase is part of a total investment strategy. Money saved is also money earned and available for investment in other securities.

Fixed-Income Investments

Most investors devote a major portion of their assets to savings. The investment of choice remains the bank CD, because of both habit and concern for preservation of capital. However, neither is a good reason to place a disproportionate amount of assets in CDs. There are many government fixed-income investments that may be considered by conservative investors. A brief overview follows.

Government Fixed-Income Investments

Refer to Table 13–4.

1. All direct and agency government obligations are subject to market risk but not credit risk. Treasury zero coupon bond prices can be volatile.

Table 13–4. Government Fixed-Income Investments

	Credit Risk	Maturity	Interest Paid	Liquidity
Treasury Bills	None	3/12 Mo.	At Maturity	Instant
Treasury Notes	None	2-10 Yr.	Six Months	Instant
Treasury Bonds	None	10-30 Yr.	Six Months	Instant
Treasury Zeros	None	1-28 Yr.	At Maturity	Instant
Government Agencies	None	1-30 Yr.	Various	Instant

2. Treasury bills, bonds, and notes may be purchased directly from the U.S. Treasury. Be assured that it is a simple and efficient process. Call your nearest Federal Reserve Bank and ask for the Treasury Direct Tender forms. Also ask for the instruction pamphlets.

3. Government securities offer good liquidity. Securities sold prior to maturity may have higher or lower prices than the original purchase price. To receive the best total return, 13-, 26-, and 52-week Treasury bills and 2- and 5-year Treasury notes should be held until maturity.

Fixed Annuities Versus Certificates of Deposit (CDs)

There are certain circumstances in which fixed annuities are appropriate for investors. The primary purpose of a variable or fixed annuity remains to provide wealth accumulation and retirement and/or estate assets. Often, fixed annuities can address those needs.

During periods of high interest rates for fixed annuities and government securities, an investor may want to "lock in" or guarantee the return of the fixed-income portion of a long-term, diversified investment strategy. As an example, a 7 to 8% riskless return guaranteed for an extended time period is hard to resist. The considerations for investing are time horizon, liquidity, and asset allocation. In Table

13–5, the fixed-income investments have varying maturities and provide excellent liquidity options—scenario hard to resist.

Keep in mind, though, the possibility of current taxes on the government securities and potential fixed annuity contingent deferred sales charges (CDSC).

Table 13–6 provides a comparison of the distinguishing features of fixed annuities and CDs. Guaranteed return of principal is an emotional rather than a logical issue with long-term investors. All investors are willing to step forward and accept a more competitive return. The ranks diminish quickly if the higher reward requires

Table 13–5

Example: A $100,000 portfolio seeks long-term growth and diversification using an asset-allocation mix of 60% equities and 40% fixed-income.

40% Fixed-Income Allocation*

$10,000	U.S. Government	5-Year	7.50% Note
$10,000	U.S. Government	2-Year	6.75% Note
$20,000	Fixed Annuity	5-Year	7.50% Guaranteed Rate

*For illustration purposes only.

The total riskless weighted return is 7.31% with an average maturity of 4.25 years.

Table 13–6

Feature Comparison	Fixed Annuities	CDs
Guaranteed Investment Return	Yes	Yes
Interest Rate Guaranteed	Yes	Yes
Early Withdrawal Penalty	Yes	Yes
IRS Early Withdrawal Penalty	Yes	No
Long-Term Investment	Yes	No
Address Inflation Concerns	No	No

adding risk. Should an investor accept risk? Two schools of thought exist. The logic behind assuming market risk is: over the long term risk dissipates, nonguaranteed securities outperform guaranteed securities, equities outperform bonds, and the biggest risk an investor faces is inflation. The logic behind guaranteed investments is: fixed annuities are commendable investments when fixed rates are competitive; the time horizon is 10 years or less; the preservation of capital is paramount; and the investor is not comfortable accepting meaningful risk.

Summary

- One of the most important investments for individuals and families is a home. Aside from the pride of ownership and emotional security, purchasing a home offers tax advantages, long-term capital gains, and deferred wealth accumulation.
- There are disadvantages to real estate investing: during periods of recession and deflation home values can decrease. Also, real estate lacks liquidity and is expensive and time-consuming to sell.
- Annuities and mutual funds are kindred spirits in the world of investing. Each offers many of the same advantages, particularly professional money management and competitive growth. Their primary difference is the method of taxation.
- Municipal bonds, mutual funds, and variable annuities make a terrific combination for long-term wealth accumulation.
- Life insurance is a simple concept. It offers protection for an individual's family, business, or other defined risk. There are two types of life insurance: term and ordinary. Each offers protection. Ordinary combines protection with savings and investment features. Should an investor purchase ordinary life or purchase term and invest the difference? For sophisticated investors term is usually the better answer.

- Universal variable life offers competitive returns and separate account investing that includes stocks, bonds, and cash. It also charges higher expenses. Before purchasing universal life, an evaluation of return versus cost is recommended.
- When interest-rate guarantees are competitive, fixed annuity and government securities can make a very competitive credit-risk-free investment combination.
- Certificates of deposit (CDs) are not an appropriate approach to long-term investing. Assuming even modest risk greatly improves an investor's total return versus CDs.

14

A SUMMARY ANALYSIS OF VARIABLE ANNUITIES AND THEIR INCLUSION IN A COMPREHENSIVE FINANCIAL PLAN

KEY CONCEPTS

▼ The Importance of a Well-Designed Investment Program

▼ The Dynamic Opportunities Offered by Variable Annuities

▼ (Q + T + C) Investing

▼ The Myths of Retirement Planning

Our recurring theme throughout this book has been to develop a comprehensive investment strategy. That includes considering a copious number of investments to build a synergistic, diversified portfolio.

Many individuals lack a clear understanding of investments and their potential for wealth accumulation. Intuitively the importance of attaining certain financial goals is clearly understood. However, few individuals have the sophistication to implement a program that includes consistent performance, competitive returns, risk reduction, and diversification.

Conservative investors focus on the preservation of capital as their primary investment objective, while ignoring the indisputable adverse consequences of inflation. Avoiding market risk brings investors emotional satisfaction. They assume their assets are "safe." However, eliminating risk eliminates the opportunity of receiving competitive and consistent returns. The goal is to receive a positive net return within the constraints of acceptable risk.

Implementing a comprehensive strategy is not difficult. By combining certain investment practices, an investor develops a climate favorable to the accumulation of wealth. Among these practices are: First, start an investment program as quickly as possible. Expanding an investment program's time horizon reduces the contribution requirements and enhances the dynamics of compounding. Second, diversify into as many tax-advantaged investments as practicable including retirement, savings, and salary-reduction plans. Third, reinvest all earnings to take full advantage of compounding. Fourth, understand that the greatest long-term risk is inflation. Finally, diversify assets to reduce risk.

Even when implementing the many obvious and elementary investment practices, few individuals possess the expertise to "pull it together" and manage their investable assets to maximize the return for the risk accepted. This lack of knowledge, when combined with another hindrance, procrastination, lessens the opportunity for success even further.

Gaining sufficient investment knowledge gives investors the ability to define their goals and objectives and understand that the approach to successful investing is straightforward. The ingredients are knowledge, discipline, consistency, time horizon, and realistic expectations.

Variable annuities offer investors a significant opportunity to use the principal ingredients of successful investing. The predominant annuity component is accumulating wealth tax-deferred. This benefit makes the "magic of compounding" very effective. The opportunity for success is further enhanced by employing talented professional money managers to manage sub-account assets. The managers generate competitive returns and reduce risk through diversification. Finally, investors control the distribution, and hence the taxation timing, of the annuity assets.

While our primary focus is on variable annuities, fixed annuities also offer definite investment advantages. Fixed annuities can be advantageous when an investment time horizon is clearly defined, competitive rates are guaranteed for an extended period, and the contingent deferred sales charges (CDSC) are reasonably structured. Fixed annuities offer the same basic features and benefits as a variable annuity. The major difference is that the fixed annuity's return is guaranteed. The variable annuity's return depends on the performance of the underlying securities in the sub-accounts. Over an extended period, variable annuity equity sub-accounts will generally outperform fixed annuity guaranteed rates.

Investing in fixed annuities requires two primary decisions: selecting a maturity date and accepting a guaranteed interest rate. As with CDs, the interest rate is a function of the interest-rate markets. Fixed annuities are structured in two basic formats: offering 1-year guaranteed rates with annual renewals or interest-rate periods guaranteed for periods ranging from 1 to 10 years. Guarantees of 1, 2, 3, 5, 7, and 10 years are common. One-year renewable rates are the industry standard.

The features and benefits of variable annuities are numerous and advantageous to investors seeking a strategy for long-term wealth accumulation. The principal benefit remains tax-deferred wealth accumulation. This is enhanced by an annuity owner's ability to reallocate between sub-accounts without creating a taxable event or being subject to commission charges.

Variable annuities have no initial sales charges; 100% of the money (contributions) is invested for the benefit of the annuity owner. The annuity also provides the owner systematic and periodic withdrawal options. These withdrawals are not subject to surrender penalties unless they exceed certain withdrawal limitations. This creates reasonable and periodic liquidity options for investors.

Variable annuities are insurance policies. A guaranteed death benefit is included as a benefit. The minimum amount paid to a beneficiary will be the greater of the total contributions or the value of the policy. Many variable annuity guaranteed death benefits are adjusted upward after a certain period. As previously stated, the author does not characterize this as a significant benefit. Its primary function is to qualify an annuity as an insurance contract which, in turn, allows the deferred benefits.

The variable annuity avoids probate. At the death of the contract owner the annuity contract will transfer to the joint owner or to the beneficiary without requiring probate. There are no delays. The beneficiary(s) has immediate access to the proceeds. However, the annuity value is still included in the deceased's estate.

The largest dollar volume of variable and fixed annuities are purchased by two clearly defined target groups. The largest investor group is 50 plus, affluent, financially secure, and conservative. They are accumulating assets for retirement and financial security. A smaller group has the same demographics except they are more affluent. Their investment objectives are to build wealth and to avoid current taxes. (A third group purchases annuities as an employment benefit. The focus of this book remains on the individual investor.)

The 50-plus affluent group and the wealthy group have concerns about gaining access to their funds in the event of financial emergencies. The ideal situation is for an investor to meet liquidity concerns with an emergency fund. However, should the need arise, annuities offer numerous disbursement options. No-penalty percentage or accumulated earnings withdrawals are an option. Partial or lump-sum withdrawals are another.

Investment Note: certain distributions may be subject to IRS tax and early withdrawal penalties. The point is: while withdrawals are not always the best solution, annuities can meet liquidity needs.

Safety is another concern of annuity investors. Fixed annuities guarantee returns. Variable annuities' returns are not guaranteed but will grow competitively over the long term. Safety concerns should also include the solvency of the insurance company issuer. Remember: the companies are highly regulated. They have stringent reserve requirements that preserve the integrity of the assets. All annuities are guaranteed by the full faith and credit of the company. In addition, variable annuity assets are held by trustees.

Other benefits include:

1. Investors may exchange contracts under Section 1035 without creating a taxable event.
2. After receipt, investors have no less than 10 days to review the contract for suitability.
3. Investors control annuity asset disbursements, thus controlling taxation.
4. While not tax-deductible, contributions for the purchase of an annuity are not limited by federal statute.
5. The sub-account assets are managed by some of the most talented money managers available.

Investing addresses the major objective of all investors: financial independence. Achieving a comfortable and secure financial status is not necessarily easy. The single biggest concern for investors remains the loss of purchasing power caused by inflation. CDs and certain other fixed-income investments that offer guaranteed rates seldom produce net positive returns (total return minus taxes minus inflation).

Assuming risk is the best method for beating inflation. Success is most probable when risk assumption is combined with other investment basics, including the "magic" of compound earnings, consistent and competitive performance, a long-term time horizon, and realistic expectations.

Before purchasing an annuity, an investor should understand the significance and importance of sub-accounts. They offer three investment opportunities: stocks, bonds, and cash. Each has a degree of risk. Stocks offer the best chance for competitive returns and beating inflation.

Variable annuity sub-accounts are the equivalent of mutual funds except they are part of an insurance contract. As with mutual funds, there are three dominant types of sub-accounts for long-term investing: equity, fixed-income (bonds), and special situations. Money market funds are used for short-term investing needs. Within the three dominant categories are subcategories that offer further diversification opportunities. The special situations sub-accounts are the most diverse. They include various types of speculative and exotic investment opportunities.

For investors unduly concerned about sub-account selection, there is solace. Dr. Harry M. Markowitz's Nobel Prize–winning effort, *Portfolio Selection and Efficient Diversification of Investments*, stresses that individual securities transactions are important only to the extent that they affect the risk-return relationship of the total portfolio. Translation: select good money managers, not individual securities.

The ultimate objective of retirement planning is to first design and then implement a plan that will systematically accumulate assets and accomplish an investor's long-term financial goal of funding retirement. Annuities offer many options to meet those objectives.

More moderately affluent investors have at least four major investment concerns: having an adequate monthly retirement income; market risk on their investments; depletion of assets for retirement living expenses; and asset liquidity for major medical and other expenses. Addressing these concerns requires planning, persistence, and professional guidance.

Wealth accumulation and retirement planning require three steps: establishing goals and objectives, implementing a long-term investment plan, and periodically monitoring and evaluating the results.

Designing and implementing an appropriate financial plan is not difficult: Financial Goals + Types of Investments + Time Line + Funding Methods = Financial Planning. Before making any decisions, investors should determine their net worth, estimated future earnings, time horizon, current expenses, retirement needs, cash flow, and any special circumstances needing attention.

The most open question and the least quantifiable answer is, after retirement, what income is required to maintain your present standard of living?

We have previously discussed a number of misconceptions about retirement and retirement planning, but one bears repeating, especially that the biggest risk retirees face is inflation. Retirement plans can provide a significant amount of the estimated 80% of your present income required to maintain your standard of living during retirement. Qualified retirement plans offer powerful incentives for employers to establish and for employees to participate in retirement plans: immediate tax deductions and tax-deferred wealth accumulation. I recommend that working individuals eligible to participate in qualified plans contribute the maximum allowable amount unless mitigating circumstances prevent it. For some plans the contributions are excluded from income (401(k) type). Others are tax-deductible (IRA type). Contributions from employers are not included in an employee's current income. Retirement plans are a great deal!

Once investors maximize their contributions to retirement plans, the next investment might be a variable annuity. Investment knowledge is power: purchasing an annuity must be an informed and systematic undertaking.

Unless an investor strongly favors the purchase of a no-load variable annuity, the first order of business is to select an investment advisor to assist in the selection. Even if one has a financial advisor, it is a good idea to discuss your proposed purchase with several other sources. (A little extra advice: the advisor should understand financial planning, investing, annuities, and asset allocation. CPAs and other tax professionals are great tax advisors but not necessarily well informed or knowledgeable investment advisors. As with taxation, investing is a highly specialized and often complicated area.)

When evaluating a variable annuity there are certain features and benefits that are important and should be offered in the contract. They include sub-account choices, money managers, surrender charges (CDSC), fees and expenses, death benefit, and distribution options. This selection and evaluation process can be greatly enhanced by using various research sources, including *Morningstar Variable Annuity Performance Report*. Research should take a top-down approach. First, analyze the insurance company sponsoring the contract. Determine its quality, stability, and reputation. Second, review the sub-accounts' long-term performance and diversification options. Finally, review the individual features and benefits of the contract.

Evaluating sub-accounts is tedious. Other than performance, consider whether there are sufficient alternatives to meet diversification and asset-allocation requirements. There is no "correct" number of sub-accounts. However, attention must be focused on the equity sub-accounts, the true strength of variable annuities.

Variable annuity investing is also tax-advantaged investing. When included in a strategy with qualified retirement plans and municipal bonds, an investor has implemented a three-tiered, diversified investment approach. We have discussed combining retirement plans and variable annuities in a synergistic investment approach. Now we will include municipal bonds as the third component.

Investors purchase municipal bonds for one reason: tax-free income. With retirement plans and variable annuities, the income is tax-deferred. With municipal bonds, what you see is what you get.

Investment Note: Many states levy taxes on out-of-state municipal bond income.

Municipal bonds are appropriate for most affluent investors. The immediate test for purchasing municipal bonds is the tax-free equivalent yield. One must determine which is better: a taxable yield minus taxes or the tax-free yield. Additional considerations are ratings, maturity, liquidity, and capital appreciation potential. The bottom line is that well-diversified and well-coordinated tax-advantaged investment strategies usually include variable annuities, retirement plans, and municipal bonds.

Another long-term, tax-deferred, wealth-accumulation opportunity exists with equity mutual funds and individual growth stocks. Gains are tax-deferred until the stocks are sold.

Individuals use asset allocation in their everyday lives by distributing assets in order of their priorities. Necessary and essential expenses are paid first, followed by discretionary and variable spending expenses. Investing is a discretionary asset-allocation function. The decisions include short- or long-term time investment horizon, amount for each investment category, and the regularity of contributions. Asset allocation as it relates to variable annuities deals with stocks, bonds, and cash. Diversification addresses allocation among specific security classifications. Asset allocation and diversification produce more consistent and more competitive returns. However, the true test of both approaches remains meeting investor needs.

Understanding the direct relationship between risk and reward is as important as understanding asset allocation and diversification.

For every unit of risk assumed, an additional unit of reward should be received. By definition, risk is the exposure to the chance of loss.

Investment risk is measurable. Beta measures risk. Alpha measures return. Understanding beta is simple yet important. It gives an investor a "measuring stick" when comparing various variable annuity sub-accounts.

Standard deviation is another excellent benchmark. However, investors need not make extensive calculations to appreciate its value. The major benefit is understanding that with 68% certainty (one standard deviation) an investor can know the worst-, best-, and expected-case scenarios of particular investments. Research investment services provide this information.

Understanding a variable annuity prospectus is also important to investors. Contrary to popular belief, a prospectus is readable, relatively easy to understand, and is an invaluable tool for educating investors on the features and specifics of the contract.

The major concern of most investors remains the preservation of capital. This is particularly true of CD buyers. They are willing to accept higher rates but unwilling to accept risk. It is a matter of education—reasonable risk equals higher returns. Another common investment mistake is funding long-term investment goals with short-term investments. Most unreasonable or unrealistic fears can be overcome by a commonsense approach to investing: never purchase an investment from someone you don't know well; have realistic return expectations. More investors have lost money "reaching" for yields than through any other investor mistake. Investors should never forget that quality is important.

The formula for investing success remains quality investments plus time horizon plus compounding (Q + T + C). It is important not to confuse time with market timing: only one works, and it is not market timing. Temperament is important, but patience is the most important virtue of all.

While we have focused on tax-advantaged securities' investing, there are other alternatives available for individual wealth accumulation. The most attractive is home ownership. With rare exceptions, there is no investment more financially or emotionally rewarding than owning a home. The interest payments and real estate taxes are deductible. Over time, homes appreciate in value. All the gains are tax-deferred until the home is sold.

Another investment to be considered is mutual funds. As previously discussed, municipal bonds and growth stocks can be purchased through mutual funds. Mutual funds are not tax-advantaged in the sense of annuities and retirement plans, unless they are included as retirement plan options.

However, they offer professional management, competitive returns, and more investment options than any other investment group. Mutual funds and annuities are complementary, not mutually exclusive investments. The only significant difference between the two is that, in variable annuity contracts, mutual funds are called sub-accounts.

Another category, life insurance, should be closely reviewed by investors. The critical question is, What is the purpose of insurance? The answer is pure protection and transferring an individual's risk to an insurance company. In the view of this author, purchasing pure coverage is the appropriate choice.

Under certain conditions, there is an investment use for fixed annuities. When rate guarantees are competitive and available for extended time periods, fixed annuities can be very attractive investments. Also, combining fixed annuity rates with short- to medium-term U.S. government notes (two to five years) can make a very competitive, credit-risk-free investment combination.

Finally, certificates of deposit (CDs) are not appropriate for long-term investing. Assuming even modest risk greatly improves an investor's total return as compared to CDs.

EVALUATION SERVICES

A. M. Best Co., Inc.
Ambest Road
Oldwick, NJ 08858
908-439-2200

Lipper Analytical Securities Corporation
74 Trinity Place
New York, NY 10006–2002
212-393-1300

Moody's Investors Service
99 Church Street
New York, NY 10007
212-553-0300

Morningstar Inc.
Morningstar Variable Annuity Performance Report
225 W. Wacker Drive, Suite 400
Chicago, IL 60606–1228
312-696-6000

Standard & Poor's Ratings Group
McGraw Hill
1221 Avenue of the Americas
New York, NY 10020–1095
212-512-2000

Value Line Inc.
220 E. 42nd Street, 6th Floor
New York, NY 10017–5806
212-907-1500

SOURCES

Issuing Insurance Company

Aetna Life Insurance & Annuity Company
151 Farmington Avenue
Hartford, CT 01656
800-238-6263

AIG Life Insurance Company
One Alico Plaza
600 King Street
Wilmington, DE 19801
800-441-7468

Allianz Life Insurance Company
1750 Hennepin Avenue South
Minneapolis, MN 55403
800-328-5600

Allmerica Financial Services, Inc.
(State Mutual)
440 Lincoln St.
Worcester, MA 01605
800-622-9876

American Express Life Insurance Company
IDS Tower 10
Minneapolis, MN 55440
612-671-3131

American General Life Insurance Company
Box 1401
Houston, TX 77251
800-231-3655

American International Life Insurance Company
80 Pine Street
New York, NY 10005
212-770-7000

American Life Insurance Company of NY
666 Fifth Avenue
New York, NY 10103
800-872-5963

American Republic Life Insurance Company
601 6th Avenue
Des Moines, IA 50334
800-247-2190

American Skandia Life Insurance Company
Tower One, Corporate Drive
Shelton, CT 06484
800-541-3087

American United Life Insurance Company
One American Square
Indianapolis, IN 46204
800-634-1629

Ameritas Variable Life Insurance Company
5900 "O" Street
Lincoln, NE 68510
800-745-1112

Anchor National Life Insurance Company
1999 Avenue of the Stars
Los Angeles, CA 90067
800-445-7861

AUSA Life Insurance Company
4 Manhattan Road
Purchase, NY 10577
914-697-8000

Bankers Security Life Insurance Company
4601 North Fairfax Drive
Arlington, VA 22203
800-228-4725

Canada Life Insurance Company
6201 Powers Ferry Road, NW #600
Atlanta, GA 30339
800-333-2542

Canada Life Insurance Company of NY
500 Mamaroneck Avenue
Harrison, NY 10528
914-835-8400

Century Life Insurance Company
200 Heritage Way
Waverly, IA 50677
800-798-6600

Charter Life Insurance Company
8301 Maryland Avenue
St. Louis, MO 63105
800-325-8405

Connecticut General Life Insurance Company
Hartford, CT 06152
203-726-6000

CNA Insurance
CNA Plaza 333 Wabash
Chicago, IL 60685
312-822-5000

Equitable Life Insurance Society of the U.S.
787 Seventh Avenue
New York, NY 10019
800-628-6673

Farm Bureau Life Insurance Company
5400 University Avenue
West Des Moines, IA 50266
800-247-4170

Fidelity Investments Life Insurance Company
82 Devonshire St.
Boston, MA 02109
800-544-2422

Fidelity Stand Life Insurance Company
11365 West Olympic Blvd.
Los Angeles, CA 90064
800-283-4536

Financial Horizons Life Insurance Company
Box 182008
Columbus, OH 43218–2008
800-533-5622

First Investors Life Insurance Company
99 Wall Street
New York, NY 10005
800-832-7783

First SunAmerica Life Insurance Company
733 Third Avenue
New York, NY 10017
800-272-3007

First Transamerica Life Insurance Company
575 Fifth Avenue
New York, NY 10017–2422
800-258-4260

First Variable Life Insurance Company
361 Whitney Avenue
Holyoke, MA 01040
800-544-0086

Fortis Benefits Life Insurance Company
Box 64271
St Paul, MN 55164
612-738-4000

General American Life Insurance Company
Box 66821
St. Louis, MO 63166–6821
800-237-6580

Golden American Life Insurance Company
Box 66821
St. Louis, MO 63166–6821
800-366-0066

Great American Reserve Insurance Company
11815 North Pennsylvania Street
Carmen, NY 46032
800-824-2726

Great-Western Life and Annuity Company
8515 E. Orchard Road
Englewood, CO 80111
800-468-8661

Guardian Life Insurance Company
201 Park Avenue South
New York, NY 10003
800-221-3253

Hartford Life Insurance Company
Box 2999
Hartford, CT 06104–2999
800-862-6668

Integrity Life Insurance Company
551 Madison Avenue, 11th Floor
New York, NY 10022
800-325-8583

Jefferson-Pilot Life Insurance Company
100 North Greene Street
Greensboro, NC 27401
910-691-3000

John Hancock Mutual Life Insurance Company
John Hancock Place, Box 111
Boston, MA 02117
800-255-5291

Kemper Investors Life Insurance Company
120 South LaSalle Street
Chicago, IL 60603
800-621-1048

Keyport Life Insurance Company
125 High Street
Boston, MA 02110–2712
800-437-4466

Life Insurance Company of Virginia
6610 West Broad Street
Richmond, VA 23230
800-628-2238

Lincoln Benefit Life Insurance Company
206 South 13th Street
Lincoln, NE 68508
800-865-5237

Lincoln National Life Insurance Company
1300 South Clinton Street
Fort Wayne, IN 46801
800-942-5500

Lutheran Brotherhood Variable Insurance Products Corp.
625 Fourth Avenue, South
Minneapolis, MN 55415
800-328-4552

Manufacturer's Life Insurance Company
200 Bloor Street, East
Toronto, Ontario, Canada M4W 1E5
800-827-4546

MassMutual Life Insurance Company
1295 State Street
Springfield, MA 01111
800-877-7084

Merrill Lynch Life Insurance Company
800 Sudders Mill Road
Plainsboro, NJ 08536
609-282-2067

Metropolitan Life Insurance Company
One Madison Avenue
New York, NY 10010
800-553-4459

Midland National Life Insurance Company
One Midland Plaza
Sioux Falls, SD 57193
605-335-5700

Minnesota Mutual Life Insurance Company
400 North Robert Street
St. Paul, MN 55101
800-443-3677

MONY Life Insurance Company of America
1740 Broadway
New York, NY 10019
National Home Life Assurance Company
800-487-6669

Mutual of America Life Insurance Company
666 Fifth Avenue
New York, NY 10103
800-467-3785

National Home Life Assurance Company
20 Moores Road
Frazer, PA 19355
800-522-5555

National Home Life Assurance Company of NY
520 Columbia Drive
Johnson City, NY 13790
800-252-1053

National Integrity Life Insurance Company
551 Madison Avenue
New York, NY 10022
800-433-1778

Nationwide Life Insurance Company
One Nationwide Plaza
Columbus, OH 43215–2220
800-848-6331

New England Mutual Life Insurance Company
501 Boylston Street
Boston, MA 02117
617-578-3500

New York Life Insurance & Annuity Corporation
51 Madison Avenue
New York, NY 10010
212-576-7000

Northwestern Mutual Life Insurance Company
720 East Wisconsin Avenue
Milwaukee, WI 53202
412-271-1444

Northwestern National Life Insurance Company
20 Washington Avenue
Minneapolis, MN 55401
612-372-5432

North American Security Life Insurance Company
116 Huntington Avenue
Boston, MA 02116
617-266-6004

Northbrook Life Insurance Company
3100 Sanders Road
Northbrook, IL 60062
800-654-2397

Ohio National Life Insurance Company
237 William Howard Taft Road
Cincinnati, OH 45219
800-366-6654

Pacific Mutual Life Insurance Company
700 Newport Center Drive
Newport Beach, CA 92660
800-800-7681

Painewebber Life Insurance Company
601 6th Avenue
Des Moines, IA 50309
N/A

PFL Life Insurance Company
4333 Edgewood Road, N.E.
Cedar Rapids, IA 52499
800-247-3615

Phoenix Home Life Insurance Company
One American Row
Hartford, CT 06102–5056
800-892-4885

Principal Mutual Life Insurance Company
711 High Street
Des Moines, IA 50392–0001
800-247-4123

Protective Life Insurance Company
2801 Highway 280 South
Birmingham, AL 35223
800-866-3555

Provident Mutual Life and Annuity Company
1600 Market Street
Philadelphia, PA 19103
800-654-7796

Prudential Insurance Company
Five Prudential Plaza
Newark, NJ 07101
201-802-6000

Safeco Life Insurance Company
Safeco Plaza
Seattle, WA 98185
800-426-7649

Security Benefit Life Insurance Company
700 Harrison Street
Topeka, KS 66636
800-888-2461

Security First Life Insurance Company
11365 Olympic Blvd.
Los Angeles, CA 90064
800-284-4536

State Mutual Life Assurance Company
400 Lincoln Street
Worcester, MA 01653–1959
800-533-7881

Sun Life Assurance Company of Canada
One Sun Life Executive Park
Wellesley, MA 01281
800-225-3950

Teachers Insurance & Annuity Association
730 Third Avenue
New York, NY 10017
800-842-2733

Templeton Funds Annuity Company
700 Central Avenue
St. Petersburg, FL 33733–8030
813-823-8712

Transamerica Occidental Life Insurance Company
1150 South Oliver Street
Los Angeles, CA 90015
N/A

Travelers Insurance Company
One Tower Square
Hartford, CT 06183–1051
800-842-0125

United Central Life Insurance Company
Box 179
Cincinnati, OH 45201
800-825-1551

United Investors Life Insurance Company
2001 Third Avenue, South
Birmingham, AL 35233
205-325-4300

USAA Life Insurance Company
9800 Fredericksburg Road
San Antonio, TX 78288
N/A

Variable Annuity Life Insurance Company
Box 3206
Houston, TX 77253
713-465-2253

Western Reserve Life Insurance Company
201 Highland Avenue
Largo, FL 34640
800-443-9975

WM Life Insurance Company
Box 370
Seattle, WA 98111
800-882-8003

Xerox Financial Services Insurance Company
One Tower Lane #3000
Oakbrook Terrace, IL 60181
800-523-1661

The author wishes to express his deep appreciation to *Lipper Analytical Services, Inc.*, Denver, Colorado, and their highly professional staff for furnishing the names and addresses of the numerous vendors of variable annuities listed above. Again, thank you *Lipper Analytical Services, Inc.*, for your assistance and tremendous support.

INDEX

ABOUT THE AUTHOR

Bruce Franklin Wells is a nationally recognized sales trainer, motivational speaker, humorist, writer, and investment expert in the financial services industry. He is the founder and Senior Managing Director of the Institute of Certified Investment Specialists, an investment consulting and sales and training group to banks, insurance companies, and brokerage firms. He resides, writes, and maintains a permanent tan on the beaches of Gulf Breeze, Florida.